Cottage-Style Quilts

16 Projects for Casual Country Living

Mary Hickey

Martingale®
& C O M P A N Y

Dedication

Few people could exhibit the patience and kindness shown by my husband, Phil, in the last year. He has hauled tons of fabric and sewing machines up and down stairs and in and out of the car, proofread instructions, prepared meals, fixed the computer, and cleaned the house. This dear, kind man even learned to hand stitch bindings and hanging sleeves to make my life easier. He has never complained and always encouraged and cheered me on. What a guy! Thirty-eight years of marriage and he is still a solid rock of kindness!

Acknowledgments

A year ago this book was just a kernel of an idea. Now, thanks to the encouragement of Nancy Martin, Mary Green, and Karen Soltys, it is a reality.

Many thanks to:

Cleo Nollette for her friendship, encouragement, and cat quilt, "Cleo's Cats."

Dawn Kelly and Judy Irish, professional machine quilters whose magic stitches brought so many of the quilts to life. They are both such gifted and generous artists.

Fannie Schwartz, whose fine hand quilting brought "Helen's Wreaths" to life.

Moda Fabrics, whose lovely fabrics created so many of the quilts.

The staff at Martingale & Company that makes authors look so good!

And most of all, Phil Hickey, who did so much work with such grace.

Credits

President ▪ Nancy J. Martin
CEO ▪ Daniel J. Martin
Publisher ▪ Jane Hamada
Editorial Director ▪ Mary V. Green
Managing Editor ▪ Tina Cook
Technical Editor ▪ Laurie Baker
Copy Editor ▪ Durby Peterson
Design Director ▪ Stan Green
Illustrators ▪ Brian Metz and Laurel Strand
Cover Designer ▪ Stan Green
Text Designer ▪ Shelly Garrison
Photographer ▪ Brent Kane

That Patchwork Place® is an imprint of Martingale & Company®.

Cottage-Style Quilts: 16 Projects for Casual Country Living
© 2005 by Mary Hickey

Martingale & Company
20205 144th Avenue NE
Woodinville, WA 98072-8478 USA
www.martingale-pub.com

Printed in China
10 09 08 07 06 05   8 7 6 5 4 3 2 1

Library of Congress Cataloging-in-Publication Data

Hickey, Mary.
 Cottage-style quilts : 16 projects for casual country living / Mary Hickey.
  p. cm.
  ISBN 1-56477-587-9
1. Patchwork—Patterns. 2. Quilting—Patterns.
3. Cottages in art. I. Title.
  TT835.H4525 2005
  746.46'041—dc22
                                   2004024672

Mission Statement

Dedicated to providing quality products and service to inspire creativity.

Contents

Introduction

For some people the word "cottage" evokes the vision of a small shuttered getaway at the lake or a little farmhouse in the country. For others a cottage is a hideaway in the garden or in the mountains. Whatever comes to mind for you, all cottages share some basic characteristics: primarily a sense of coziness, a special feeling of warmth and welcoming, and an air of informality.

Of course, you don't have to live in a cottage to decorate your home in this relaxed style. Cottage-style decor uses a miscellaneous mix of patterns, colors, and designs to convey an easygoing, open attitude that can be adapted to any home anywhere. The depth and scope of this style make it an appropriate choice for homes hugging the seashore, sitting in the heart of the city, resting along a country lane, or perched high in the mountains.

Some simple changes to the rooms in your home may be all you need to transform your space and give it the warmth and comfort of cottage style. With their creative patterns and vivid color combinations, quilts are a natural place to start. Striking patterns and soft tactile fabrics can create the unpretentiousness of cottage style instantly. Add some painted, old, or slipcovered furniture; toss in a mixture of floral, checked, and plaid fabrics; arrange some odds and ends with family mementos and you are on your way. I remember how delighted I felt when I first realized that decorating our family home like this actually fit into a category with the name "cottage style." Because I am a quilt designer, teacher, and author, our house was rich with quilts and an eclectic blend of thrift store and garage sale furniture and accessories. What a joy to find out there was an official name for this style of decorating that we had always called "early Salvation Army."

I've carefully chosen and honed the designs in this book to give them a down-to-earth spirit and traditional flavor. At the same time, I've worked to give each design a sense of originality and freshness that will spark your imagination and nudge you to try something unpredictable or perhaps a little bit quirky.

Four distinct cottage styles are included in this book: the tiny garden cottage, the cool and breezy beach cottage, the rural farm retreat, and the cozy mountain cabin. The quilt designs are easy, straightforward blocks with simple piecing techniques. Feel free to mix the color combinations of one quilt with the block designs of another and the borders of a third. And keep in mind that the informality of cottage style allows for a few imperfections in your piecing.

Quiltmaking Techniques

All of the special techniques needed to make your quilts are covered in this section.

Half-Square-Triangle Units

These units are formed when two triangles are joined to make a square. You can cut two triangles and sew them together, but when you have a lot of units to make from the same two fabrics, this method is quicker, easier, and more accurate.

1. Refer to the quilt instructions to cut two squares of contrasting fabric. Layer the squares right sides up. Place the layered fabrics on your cutting mat.

2. Cut the squares diagonally from corner to corner. Then cut bias strips the width given in the quilt instructions. The strip width will be ½" larger than the size of the finished square.

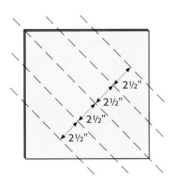

3. With right sides together, sew the strips into a unit, alternating the colors. Offset the tops exactly ¼" so that the top of the unit of strips forms a straight line. Press the seams toward

the darker strips. Repeat with the remaining strips to make a second unit.

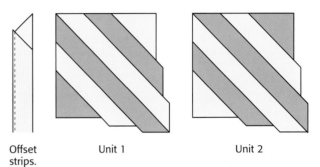

Offset strips.   Unit 1   Unit 2

4. To cut the squares from each unit, begin by rotating the unit so the straight edge is on the left as shown. Place the bias line of a Bias Square® ruler on one of the middle seam lines of one of the units. Align your long ruler with the bias ruler and trim the edge of the unit so that the cut is at a perfect 45° angle to the seam line.

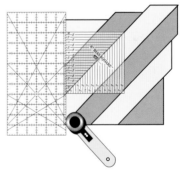

5. Cut a strip from the unit that is ½" wider than the finished square. The quilt instructions will tell you how wide to cut the strip.

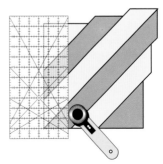

6. Repeat steps 4 and 5 to trim the edge, and then cut another strip. Continue in this manner until you have cut the entire unit into strips.

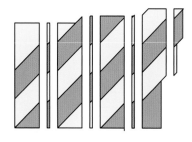

7. Lay one strip horizontally on your mat. Align the edge of the Bias Square ruler with the edge of the strip and the bias line on the ruler with the far right seam. Cut on the right side of the ruler. Position your ruler on the next seam to the left as described above; cut on the right side of the ruler. Continue in this manner until you have cut as many squares as possible from the strip. Be sure you keep all of the edges that were just cut facing the same direction. Repeat with the remaining strips.

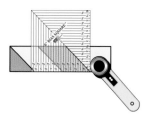

8. Turn the squares so that all of the right-hand cuts are on the left.

9. Position the ruler on each square so the diagonal line is on the seam line and the edge of the ruler is at the bottom edge of the square; trim the pieces to perfect squares.

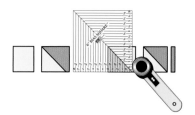

Appliqué Methods

Appliqué involves turning under the edges of shapes and sewing them to a larger piece of fabric. Resourceful quilters have developed many clever methods to accomplish this time-honored quiltmaking technique. The methods that follow are my favorites for the simple shapes used in this book.

Face-and-Turn Appliqué

1. Trace the appliqué pattern onto template plastic, cardboard, or card stock and cut out the shape. *Do not add a seam allowance.*

2. With right sides together, lay a piece of light-weight cotton or featherweight interfacing over the appliqué fabric for the backing. The backing should be approximately the same size as the appliqué fabric.

3. Place the template on the backing and trace around the shape with a water-soluble pen. Repeat to trace the desired number of shapes, leaving ½" between the shapes for a seam allowance.

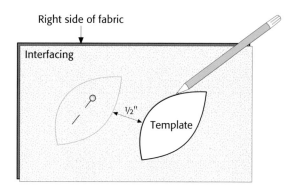

4. Using a matching-colored thread and a very short stitch length, carefully machine stitch on the marked line around all of the shapes.

5. Cut out the shapes, leaving a scant ⅛" seam allowance. In the backing of each appliqué, make a slit that is big enough to turn the piece right side out.

6. Using a spray bottle, spray the backing of each piece with water to remove the marked lines and to make it easier to smooth out the seams and points after the pieces are turned. Turn the pieces right side out and gently push out the points and curves with a knitting needle or chopstick. Press the appliqués.

7. Position the shapes on the quilt top and hand or machine appliqué them in place using your favorite method.

Fusible-Web Appliqué

Paper-backed fusible web makes quick work of making and applying appliqué shapes to your quilt top. Select a lightweight fusible web if you will be adding decorative stitching around the edges of the shapes or quilting through the shapes. If you do not plan to stitch through the shape, use a heavyweight fusible web, but be aware that the additional bonding agent can make the fused area stiff.

1. Using a pencil, trace the appliqué patterns given for the project onto the paper side of the fusible web the required number of times. Leave a small amount of space between the shapes.

Paper backing of fusible web

2. Cut around the shapes. If there is more than one cutout of a shape that will be fused to the same fabric, cut out the shapes as a group rather than individually. Fuse each shape or group of shapes to the wrong side of the appropriate fabric. Cut out each shape on the drawn line.

3. Remove the paper backing and position the shapes on the background fabric. Follow the manufacturer's instructions to fuse the appliqués in place.

4. Hand or machine stitch around the edges of each shape, if desired, using a straight, zigzag, or blanket stitch and a matching or contrasting thread.

Squaring Up the Blocks

Once you have completed the blocks for your quilt, it is time to measure them. Measure all of the blocks for your quilt. If the difference between blocks is more than $\frac{1}{16}$", you must trim all of the blocks to the smallest block size. Keep in mind that if you reduce the size of your pieced blocks, you must also reduce the size of any related pieces that make up the quilt top, such as sashing strips or setting triangles.

Do this to trim the blocks evenly:

1. Using masking tape, mark the size of the smallest block on a square ruler by adhering a piece of tape at the intersection of the horizontal and vertical measurements. In this example, we have marked the ruler at the $6\frac{1}{4}$" markings so we can trim the blocks to that size. Mark the ruler with a dot of tape at the center of the block measurement. In this example, half of $6\frac{1}{4}$" would be $3\frac{1}{8}$". Therefore, $3\frac{1}{8}$" would be the center of your block. Insert a pin through the center of the block.

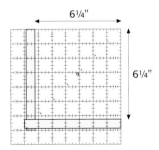
6¼"

6¼"

2. Align the center of the ruler with the center of the block and trim away the excess that extends beyond the top and right sides of the ruler. Rotate the block 180°, realign the center points, and trim the remaining two sides.

Adding Borders

Borders must be cut to fit the center measurements of the quilt. If you cut them without measuring the quilt through the center, the borders will not fit properly and will leave your quilts looking wavy or puckered. Normal stretching during construction sometimes leaves the side edges of the quilt a little longer than the center, which is why it is important to measure through the quilt-top center.

The fabric requirements for the borders in this book are based on cutting the border strips on the crosswise grain, unless otherwise indicated. Cut strips as indicated in the cutting instructions for your quilt. If the quilt is larger than the length of one strip, you will need to sew the strips together end to end, with a straight or diagonal seam, and then cut strips the exact length from the longer strip. Strips cut on the lengthwise grain will be cut longer than necessary and trimmed to size.

Borders with Straight-Sewn Corners

1. Measure the length of the quilt through the center as shown. Trim two border strips to that measurement.

2. Mark the centers of the quilt-top sides and the border strips.

3. With the centers and ends matching, stitch the strips to the sides of the quilt top, easing as necessary. Press the seams toward the borders.

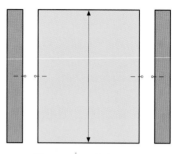

Measure top to bottom
through the center.
Mark centers.

4. Measure the width of the quilt through the center, including the side borders. Cut two strips to that measurement.

5. Mark the centers of the top and bottom edges of the quilt top and border strips. Stitch the strips to the top and bottom of the quilt top, matching the centers and ends and easing as necessary.

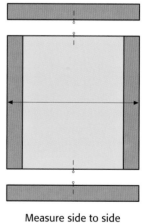

Measure side to side
through the center.
Mark centers.

6. Repeat to add any additional borders.

Borders with Corner Squares

1. Measure the length of the quilt through the center. Trim two border strips to that measurement for the sides. Measure the width of the quilt through the center and trim two border strips to that measurement for the top and bottom.

2. Stitch the side border strips to the sides of the quilt top, easing as necessary. Press the seams toward the borders.

3. Sew a corner square to each end of the top and bottom border strips and sew these units to the quilt top, easing as necessary.

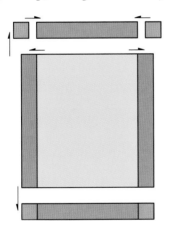

Borders with Mitered Corners

1. Measure the length of the quilt through the center and subtract ½" for seam allowances. Measure the finished *width* of the border strip. Double this measurement, and add it to the length of the quilt top. Add an extra 4". Cut two border strips to this measurement.

2. Refer to step 1 to cut the top and bottom borders, except measure the width of the quilt through the center and add the doubled width measurement of the border strips to the width of the quilt top. Don't forget to add the extra 4".

3. Cut border strips for any additional borders, being sure to add the width of the previous border strips to the measurement. If your quilt has multiple borders, center your border strips one on top of another and sew them together. This makes it easier to match the fabric at the corners and simplifies sewing the strips to the quilt top. Treat the joined multiple borders as a single unit.

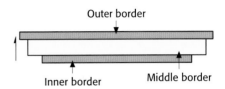

Outer border

Inner border   Middle border

4. Pencil-mark ¼" from each corner on the wrong side of the quilt top.

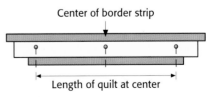

5. Using the width and length measurements of the quilt (as measured in steps 1 and 2), pin-mark the seam lines on each border strip or border unit. Fold the border strips in half and pin-mark the centers.

Center of border strip

Length of quilt at center

6. Fold the quilt top in half; use pins to mark the center of each of the sides and the top and bottom edges of the quilt.

7. Center a side border strip or unit on one side of the quilt so that the strip extends an equal distance beyond each end of the quilt top. Align the center and seam-line pins on the border with the corresponding pin and pencil marks on the quilt top; pin in place. Generously pin the rest of the border to the quilt. Make the quilt fit between the guide pins!

8. Sew the borders to the quilt top using a ¼" seam, starting and ending ¼" in from the corner of the quilt and backstitching at both ends. In other words, leave the first and last ¼" unsewn. Add the other three border strips in the same manner.

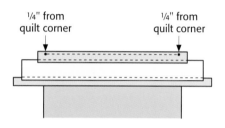

¼" from quilt corner

¼" from quilt corner

9. Fold the quilt top in half diagonally, right sides together. Arrange the border strips on either side of the corner so that they are lined up.

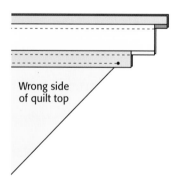

Wrong side of quilt top

10. Using a pencil and a 6" x 24" acrylic ruler with a 45° angle printed on it, mark a 45° angle on the wrong side of each strip, using your stitching line as a guide and starting at the intersection of the seam lines as shown.

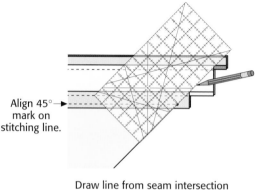

Align 45° mark on stitching line.

Draw line from seam intersection to outer edge of borders.

11. Pin carefully, matching the marked lines. Sew along the lines. Backstitch at both ends. Trim the seams to ¼" and press open.

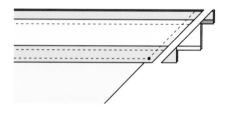

Backing

Your quilt backing should be at least 2" to 3" bigger than your quilt top on all sides. If your quilt is larger than the standard width of fabric, you will have to stitch two or more pieces of fabric together to make the backing. Remove the selvages before sewing the lengths together. Press the seams open to make quilting the top easier.

Layering and Basting

Open and unroll the batting and allow it to "relax" overnight. Press the backing and quilt top. Spread the backing wrong side up on a clean, flat surface. Use masking tape to anchor the backing to the surface without stretching the fabric. Spread the quilt batting on the backing, making sure it covers the entire backing and is smooth.

Press the top and mark it with the desired quilting design. If you are free-motion quilting or stitching in the ditch, no marking is necessary. Center the pressed and marked top on the batting and backing, right side up. Align borders and straight lines of the quilt top with the edges of the backing. Pin the layers together along the edge with large pins to hold the layers smooth.

If you will be machine quilting, use rustproof safety pins to baste the layers together. Start pinning in the center and work toward the outer edges of the quilt, spacing the pins about 4" to 6" apart. Insert the pins as you would straight pins. Avoid pinning over design lines and seam lines where you intend to stitch in the ditch. Use a needle and thread to baste a line of stitches around the outside edges. This will keep the edges from raveling while you quilt and also keep the edges aligned when you stitch the binding to the quilt. Remove the layered quilt from the hard surface, check the back to be sure it is smooth, and close the safety pins.

Hand baste around outer edge.

For hand quilting it is best to thread baste. Use a long needle and light-colored thread. If you thread your needle without cutting the thread off the spool, you will be able to baste at least two rows without rethreading your needle. Start at the center of the quilt and use large running stitches to baste across the quilt from

side to side and top to bottom. Continue basting, creating a grid of parallel lines 6" to 8" apart. Complete the basting with a line of stitches around the outside edges. This will keep the edges from raveling while you quilt and also keep the edges aligned when you stitch the binding to the quilt. After the basting is complete, remove all pins and masking tape.

Quilting

It is a personal choice as to whether you want to hand or machine quilt your quilts. If you have the time, hand quilting is a pleasurable and rewarding experience. Machine quilting should not be ignored, however. In the last few years, it has become a beautiful art form in its own right and an excellent cottage industry for many women. Practice makes perfect with either technique.

There are many excellent books available to guide you through hand and machine quilting. I urge you to consult one if you need more information.

When the quilting is complete, leave the basting stitches around the edges intact and remove the remaining basting stitches or pins. Trim the batting and backing even with the quilt top. Make sure the corners are square.

Making a Hanging Sleeve

If you are going to hang your quilt, attach a sleeve or rod pocket to the back before you bind the quilt.

1. From the leftover backing fabric, cut a piece the width of your quilt by 8". On each end, fold under a ½" hem, and then fold under ½" again; press and stitch.

2. Fold the strip in half lengthwise, wrong sides together. Stitch ¼" from the raw edges; press. With the raw edges aligned, center the tube along the top edge of the quilt top. Baste it in place. Slip-stitch the bottom edge of the sleeve to the backing fabric. When you machine stitch the binding in place you will also stitch the sleeve to the top, hiding the raw edges in the binding.

Binding Your Quilt

I like to bind my quilts with double-fold bias strips because they wear better and look smoother. However, if you have a striped fabric or other fabric with a directional design, cutting on the straight grain may give you the look you want.

1. To make bias binding strips, use the 45°-angle line on your large cutting ruler as a guide to cut enough strips to go comfortably around the quilt with about 12" extra for joining the strips and turning corners. Cut the strips 2¼" wide.

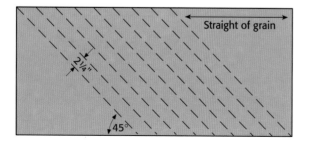

2. Join the strips as shown to make one continuous strip.

3. Press the strip in half lengthwise, wrong sides together.

4. Beginning at approximately the center of one side, align the raw edges of the folded binding with the edge of the quilt-top front. Leaving the first 10" unstitched, stitch the binding in place, stopping ¼" from the corner; backstitch. Remove the quilt from the machine.

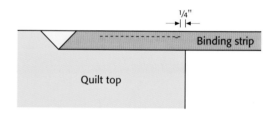

5. Fold the binding up away from the quilt so the fold forms a 45° angle. Then fold the binding back down so it is even with the next side as shown. Begin stitching at the edge of the binding and continue until you are ¼" from the next corner. Repeat this process at each corner.

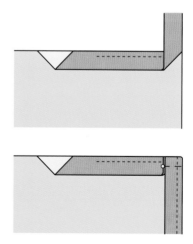

6. Stop stitching 10" from where you started. Remove the quilt from the machine and lay it on a flat surface. Fold the unstitched binding ends back on themselves so the folds just meet in the middle over the unsewn area of the quilt edge. Press the folds.

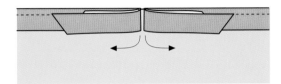

7. Unfold both ends of the binding. Open and lay the ending strip flat, right side up. Open and lay the beginning strip over it, right side down, matching the centers of the pressed Xs. Carefully draw a diagonal line through the point where the fold lines meet. Pin, and then stitch on the marked line. Check to make sure the newly seamed binding fits the unbound edge. Trim off the tail ends ¼" from the seam; press the seam open.

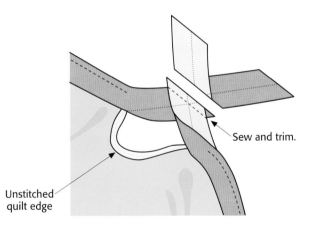

Sew and trim.

Unstitched quilt edge

8. Refold the binding, press the fold, and stitch the remainder of the binding to the quilt edge.

9. Fold the binding to the back of the quilt and blindstitch it in place using your machine stitching line as a guide and mitering the corners.

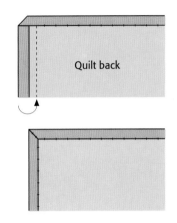

Quilt back

Adding a Quilt Label

Labeling your quilt is an important finishing touch. A label can be as simple or as elaborate as you wish. Use a plain fabric that coordinates with your backing fabric and record the name of the quilt, your name, your city and state, the date, the person who is the recipient if it is a gift, and any other interesting or important information. This can be embroidered or written with a permanent pen. If you are using a pen, iron freezer paper to the back of the fabric to stabilize it while writing.

Rosebud Quilt

By Mary Hickey. Quilted by Dawn Kelly.

One of the things I love most about spring is all the different layers and colors of green. I love the dark green of the fir trees behind the bright lime greens of new grass and budding trees, and the delicate, misty greens of ornamental fruit trees. This quilt uses several subtle shades of green to create a trellis on which the vivid rosebuds bloom. The pieces are all squares and rectangles, which makes the sewing easy.

Finished quilt size: 83" x 83"
Finished block size: 7½" x 7½"

Materials

Yardages are based on 42"-wide fabrics.

- 4¼ yards of off-white floral for background
- 2 yards of dark green fabric #1 for Chain blocks and outer border
- 1⅛ yards of light green fabric for Chain blocks and Rosebud blocks
- ¾ yard of medium green fabric for Chain blocks and Rosebud blocks
- ⅝ yard of dark rose fabric for inner border
- ⅜ yard of dark green fabric #2 for Chain blocks and Rosebud blocks
- ¼ yard *each* of light rose, light blue, light yellow, light purple, and light aqua fabrics for Rosebud blocks
- ⅛ yard *each* of medium rose, dark rose, medium blue, dark blue, medium yellow, dark yellow, medium purple, dark purple, medium aqua, and dark aqua fabrics for Rosebud blocks
- 7¼ yards of fabric for backing
- 1 yard of fabric for binding
- 86" x 86" piece of batting

Cutting

All measurements include ¼"-wide seam allowances.

From the medium green fabric, cut:
10 strips, 2" x 42"

From the off-white floral, cut:
15 strips, 2" x 42"
14 strips, 5" x 42"; crosscut 9 into 162 rectangles, 2" x 5"
6 strips, 2" x 21"
16 squares, 2" x 2"
4 strips, 8" x 42"; crosscut into 80 rectangles, 2" x 8"

From the dark green fabric #2, cut:
5 strips, 2" x 42"

From the light green fabric, cut:
14 strips, 2" x 42"
3 strips, 2" x 21"

From *each* of the medium rose, dark rose, medium blue, and dark blue fabrics, cut:
1 strip, 2" x 42"

From *each* of the light rose and light blue fabrics, cut:
2 strips, 2" x 42"

From *each* of the medium yellow, dark yellow, medium purple, dark purple, medium aqua, and dark aqua fabrics, cut:
1 strip, 2" x 21"

From *each* of the light yellow, light purple, and light aqua fabrics, cut:
2 strips, 2" x 21"

From the dark green fabric #1, cut:
8 strips, 6½" x 42"
4 strips, 2" x 42"; crosscut into:
    1 strip, 2" x 21"
    16 rectangles, 2" x 5"
    2 rectangles, 2" x 10½"

From the dark rose inner-border fabric, cut:
8 strips, 2" x 42"

From the binding fabric, cut:
342" of 2¼"-wide bias strips

Assembling the Chain Blocks

1. Sew a 2" x 42" medium green strip to both long sides of a 2" x 42" off-white strip to make strip set A. Make five strip sets. Crosscut the strip sets into 82 segments, 2" wide.

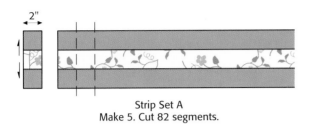

Strip Set A
Make 5. Cut 82 segments.

2. Sew a 2" x 42" off-white strip to both long sides of a 2" x 42" dark green #2 strip to make strip set B. Make three strip sets. Crosscut the strip sets into 41 segments, 2" wide.

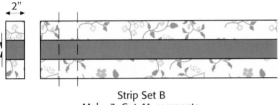
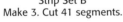

Strip Set B
Make 3. Cut 41 segments.

3. Arrange two strip set A segments and one strip set B segment as shown. Sew the segments together to make a nine-patch unit. Make 41.

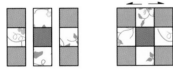

Make 41.

4. Stitch a 2" x 5" off-white rectangle to the sides of each nine-patch unit.

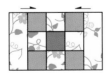

5. Stitch a 2" x 42" light green strip to both sides of a 5" x 42" off-white strip to make strip set C. Make five strip sets. Crosscut the strip sets into 82 segments, 2" wide.

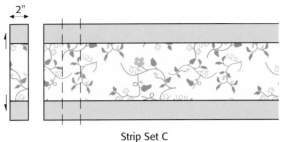

Strip Set C
Make 5. Cut 82 segments.

6. Stitch a strip set C segment to the top and bottom of each nine-patch unit to complete the Chain blocks.

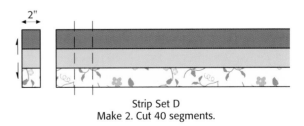

Make 41.

Assembling the Rosebud Blocks

1. Sew 2" x 42" dark green #2, light green, and off-white strips together along the long edges as shown to make strip set D. Make two. Crosscut the strip sets into 40 segments, 2" wide

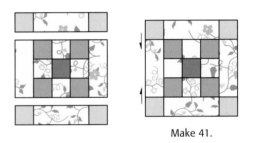

Strip Set D
Make 2. Cut 40 segments.

2. For each block color combination, sew one light-colored strip, one medium-colored strip, and one light green strip together along the long edges as shown to make strip set E. Make one strip set of each color combination. For

the rose and blue blocks, use the 2" x 42" strips. For the yellow, purple, and aqua blocks, use the 2" x 21" strips. Crosscut the strip sets into the number of 2"-wide segments shown.

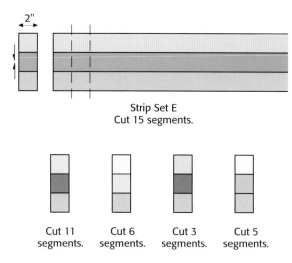

Strip Set E
Cut 15 segments.

Cut 11 segments. Cut 6 segments. Cut 3 segments. Cut 5 segments.

3. Repeat step 2 using one dark-colored strip, one light-colored strip, and one off-white strip to make strip set F.

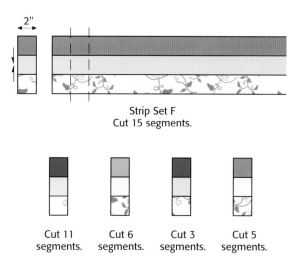

Strip Set F
Cut 15 segments.

Cut 11 segments. Cut 6 segments. Cut 3 segments. Cut 5 segments.

4. Stitch one segment *each* from strip sets D, E, and F together as shown to make the rosebud unit. Use E and F segments from the same color family.

5. Stitch a 2" x 5" off-white rectangle to the top and bottom of each rosebud unit. Stitch a

2" x 8" off-white rectangle to the sides of each rosebud unit to complete the Rosebud blocks.

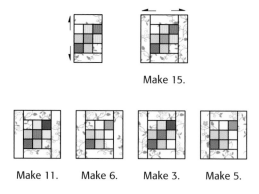

Make 15.

Make 11. Make 6. Make 3. Make 5.

Assembling the Quilt Top

1. Refer to the quilt assembly diagram to arrange the blocks into nine horizontal rows of nine blocks each, alternating the Chain and Rosebud blocks in each row and from row to row as shown. The Rosebud blocks in the featured quilt are arranged so the darkest color of the rosebud is in an upper corner and alternates from right to left in each row. The colors are randomly placed. You can place the Rosebud blocks in any position and direction you desire.

2. Stitch the blocks in each row together; press the seams toward the Chain blocks. Stitch the rows together; press the seams in one direction.

3. To make the border corner blocks, stitch a 2" x 21" off-white strip to both long sides of the 2" x 21" dark green #1 strip as shown to make strip set G. Crosscut the strip set into eight segments, 2" wide.

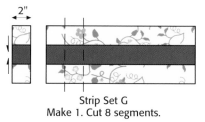

Strip Set G
Make 1. Cut 8 segments.

4. Cut the remaining 2" x 21" off-white strip in half crosswise. Stitch a 2" x 10½" dark green #1 strip to each side of one of the halves to make

strip set H. Crosscut the strip set into four segments, 2" wide.

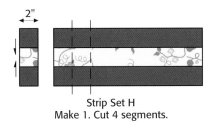

Strip Set H
Make 1. Cut 4 segments.

5. Arrange two strip set G segments and one strip set H segment as shown. Sew the segments together to make a nine-patch unit. Make four nine-patch units.

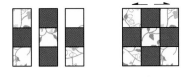

Make 4.

6. Sew a 2" x 5" dark green #1 rectangle to the sides of each nine-patch unit.

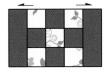

7. Stitch a 2" off-white square to the ends of the remaining eight 2" x 5" dark green #1 rectangles.

8. Stitch the units from step 7 to the top and bottom of each nine-patch unit to complete the border corner blocks.

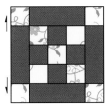

Make 4.

9. Stitch the 2" x 42" dark rose inner-border strips together end to end. Repeat with the 6½" x 42" dark green #1 strips. Stitch the rose

strip to one long side of the dark green strip. Refer to "Borders with Corner Squares" on page 9 to measure the quilt length and width and cut border strips to the required length. Refer to the quilt assembly diagram to stitch the joined border strips to the sides of the quilt top, placing the rose strip toward the inside. Stitch a border corner block to the ends of the remaining two border strips, and then stitch the strips to the top and bottom of the quilt top.

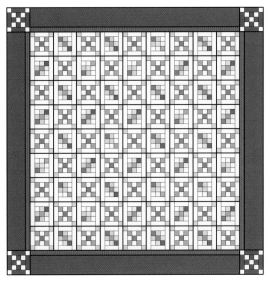

Quilt Assembly

Finishing the Quilt

Refer to "Quiltmaking Techniques" on page 5 for details on quilt finishing, if needed.

1. Cut and piece the backing fabric so it is approximately 4" to 6" larger than the quilt top.

2. Layer the backing, batting, and quilt top; baste the layers together.

3. Hand or machine quilt as desired. The quilt shown was machine quilted with rosebuds, vines, and leaves in the blocks, and a wavy feathered scroll in the borders.

4. Trim the batting and backing fabric even with the quilt top. Make a hanging sleeve and attach it to the quilt back.

5. Bind the quilt edges with the bias strips. Add a label to the quilt back.

Sunny Garden

By Mary Hickey. Quilted by Dawn Kelly.

Don't let the fabric list for this quilt scare you; just get out your shovel and start digging through your scrap box. If you look closely, you can see that each block is made up of a light, medium, and dark value of the same color. However, there is very little contrast between the values, and it is the delicacy of these contrasts that creates the gentle blending from one color to the next. The many sunny colors and the machine-appliquéd flowers in the border give this quilt the essence of a fresh, bright cottage.

Finished quilt size: 64" x 64"
Finished block size: 6" x 6"

Materials

Yardages are based on 42"-wide fabrics.

- 1½ yards of white-with-multicolored polka-dot fabric for appliquéd middle border
- 1¼ yards of dark green fabric for inner and outer borders and leaves
- 1¼ yards of medium green fabric for vines and leaves
- ½ yard of light green fabric for blocks
- ⅜ yard of dark green fabric for blocks
- ⅜ yard *each* of light pink, light periwinkle, light sky blue, light peach, and light yellow fabrics for blocks and flowers
- ¼ yard *each* of medium green, light aqua, medium aqua, dark aqua, light purple, medium purple, and dark purple fabrics for blocks
- ¼ yard *each* of medium pink, dark pink, medium periwinkle, dark periwinkle, medium sky blue, dark sky blue, medium peach, dark peach, medium yellow, and dark yellow fabrics for blocks and flowers
- ¼ yard of light green fabric for leaves
- Scrap of red fabric for centers of pink flowers
- 4 yards of fabric for backing
- ⅞ yard of fabric for binding
- 67" x 67" piece of batting
- ¼"-, ⅜"-, and ½"-wide bias bars
- 1 yard of paper-backed fusible web for fusible-web appliqué **OR** lightweight cotton or interfacing for face-and-turn appliqué

Cutting

All measurements include ¼"-wide seam allowances.

From the light green fabric for blocks, cut:
3 strips, 2" x 42"
2 strips, 3⅞" x 42"; crosscut into 12 squares, 3⅞" x 3⅞"

From the medium green fabric for blocks, cut:
3 strips, 2" x 42"

From *each* of the light pink and light periwinkle fabrics, cut:
2 strips, 2" x 42"
1 strip, 3⅞" x 42"; crosscut into 9 squares, 3⅞" x 3⅞"

From *each* of the light sky blue, light peach, and light aqua fabrics, cut:
2 strips, 2" x 42"
1 strip, 3⅞" x 42"; crosscut into 8 squares, 3⅞" x 3⅞"

From *each* of the light yellow and light purple fabrics, cut:

2 strips, 2" x 42"

1 strip, 3⅞" x 42"; crosscut into 5 squares, 3⅞" x 3⅞"

From *each* of the medium pink, medium periwinkle, medium sky blue, medium peach, medium aqua, medium yellow, and medium purple fabrics, cut:

2 strips, 2" x 42"

From the dark green fabric for blocks, cut:

2 strips, 3⅞" x 42"; crosscut into 12 squares, 3⅞" x 3⅞"

From *each* of the dark pink and dark periwinkle fabrics, cut:

1 strip, 3⅞" x 42"; crosscut into 9 squares, 3⅞" x 3⅞"

From *each* of the dark sky blue, dark peach, and dark aqua fabrics, cut:

1 strip, 3⅞" x 42"; crosscut into 8 squares, 3⅞" x 3⅞"

From *each* of the dark yellow and dark purple fabrics, cut:

1 strip, 3⅞" x 42"; crosscut into 5 squares, 3⅞" x 3⅞"

From the dark green fabric for leaves and borders, cut:

14 strips, 2" x 42"

From the polka-dot fabric, cut:

7 strips, 5¼" x 42"

From the medium green fabric for vines and leaves, cut:

250" of 1⅜"-wide bias strips

50" of 1⅛"-wide bias strips

50" of ⅞"-wide bias strips

From the binding fabric, cut:

266" of 2¼"-wide bias strips

Assembling the Sunny Garden Blocks

1. Stitch one 2" x 42" light green strip to a 2" x 42" medium green strip along the long edges to make a strip set. Repeat with the light and medium strips from the pink, periwinkle, sky blue, peach, aqua, yellow, and purple color families. Make the number of strip sets shown for each color. Press the seams toward the medium strips. Crosscut each strip set into the number of 2"-wide segments indicated above right.

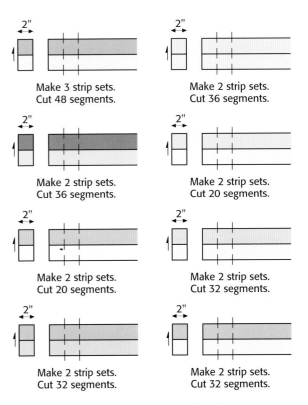

Make 3 strip sets. Cut 48 segments.

Make 2 strip sets. Cut 36 segments.

Make 2 strip sets. Cut 36 segments.

Make 2 strip sets. Cut 20 segments.

Make 2 strip sets. Cut 20 segments.

Make 2 strip sets. Cut 32 segments.

Make 2 strip sets. Cut 32 segments.

Make 2 strip sets. Cut 32 segments.

2. Stitch two segments from each color family together as indicated to make a four-patch unit. Make the number indicated for each color family.

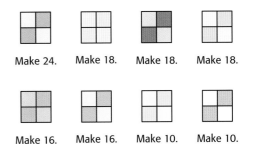

Make 24.   Make 18.   Make 18.   Make 18.

Make 16.   Make 16.   Make 10.   Make 10.

3. Using a pencil and your rotary-cutting ruler, draw a diagonal line from corner to corner on the wrong side of each 3⅞" light square. Place each marked square on a dark square from the same color family, right sides together. Stitch ¼" from each side of the marked line. Cut the squares apart on the marked line. Press the seams toward the dark color. Each pair will yield two half-square triangles.

4. Arrange two half-square triangles and two four-patch units from the same color family into two rows as shown. Stitch the units in each row together and then stitch the rows together to complete the block. Repeat with the remaining units to make the number of blocks indicated for each color family.

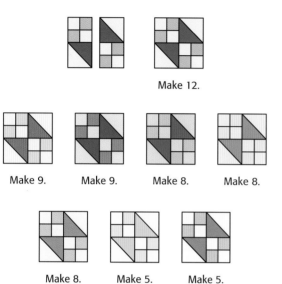

Make 12.

Make 9. Make 9. Make 8. Make 8.

Make 8. Make 5. Make 5.

Assembling the Quilt Top

1. Refer to the photo on page 22 to arrange the blocks into eight horizontal rows of eight blocks each. Rotate every other block 90° so the four-patch units form diagonal lines across the finished quilt top.

2. Stitch the blocks in each row together; press the seams in alternate directions from row to row. Stitch the rows together; press the seams in one direction.

3. Refer to "Adding Borders" on page 8 to stitch the 2" x 42" dark green border strips to-gether end to end. Repeat with the 5¼" x 42" polka-dot strips. From the pieced dark green strip, cut four 2" x 52" strips for the inner borders and four 2" x 68" strips for the outer

borders. From the polka-dot strip, cut four 5¼" x 66" strips for the middle borders. Fold the strips in half crosswise to find the center points; crease the edges. With the center points aligned, sew an inner-, middle-, and outer-border strip together as shown, matching the center points. Make four border units.

Center line

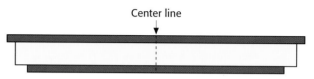

4. Stitch the 1⅜"-wide medium green bias strips together to make one long strip. Follow the manufacturer's instructions to use the ½"-wide bias bar to make a bias tube. Cut the tube into four 60" lengths. In the same manner, stitch the 1⅛"-wide bias strips together and use the ⅜"-wide bias bar to make a tube. Cut the tube into eight 5" lengths. Repeat with the ⅞"-wide bias strips and the ¼"-wide bias bar. Cut the tube into eight 5" lengths. The strips will finish to the width of the bias bars.

5. With the border unit and bias tube centers aligned, pin a ½"-wide bias tube to each border unit as shown in the illustration below. Refer to the photo as needed to pin the ⅜"-wide bias tubes in place for the red flower stems and the ¼"-wide bias tubes in place for the bluebell stems. Using matching green thread, topstitch along both long edges of each bias tube. Use a basting stitch at the beginning and end of each ½"-wide vine and a normal stitch length for the remainder of the vine and stems. After the borders have been stitched to the quilt, you can easily pluck out a few stitches and match the vines perfectly at the mitered corners, if needed, and then re-topstitch the vines in place.

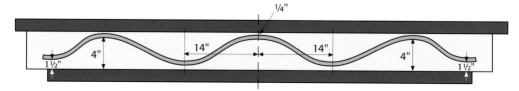

6. Refer to "Appliqué Methods" on page 6 to make the appliqué shapes and apply them to the vines and stems using patterns A–I below and the desired appliqué method. Refer to the quilt assembly diagram at right and the photo on page 22 for placement as needed.

7. Refer to "Borders with Mitered Corners" on page 9 and the quilt assembly diagram at right to stitch the appliquéd border units to the quilt top and prepare the mitered corners. Before you stitch the corners, check to be sure the vines meet in the corners; if not, pluck out a few stitches on the vines and move the vines so that they meet. Finish mitering the corners.

Finishing the Quilt

Refer to "Quiltmaking Techniques" on page 5 for details on quilt finishing, if needed.

1. Cut and piece the backing fabric so it is approximately 4" to 6" larger than the quilt top.

2. Layer the backing, batting, and quilt top; baste the layers together.

3. Hand or machine quilt as desired. The quilt shown was machine quilted with ovals, loops, flowers, vines, leaves, and swags.

4. Trim the batting and backing fabric even with the quilt top. Make a hanging sleeve and attach it to the quilt back.

5. Bind the quilt edges with the bias strips. Add a label to the quilt back.

Quilt Assembly

Appliqué Patterns

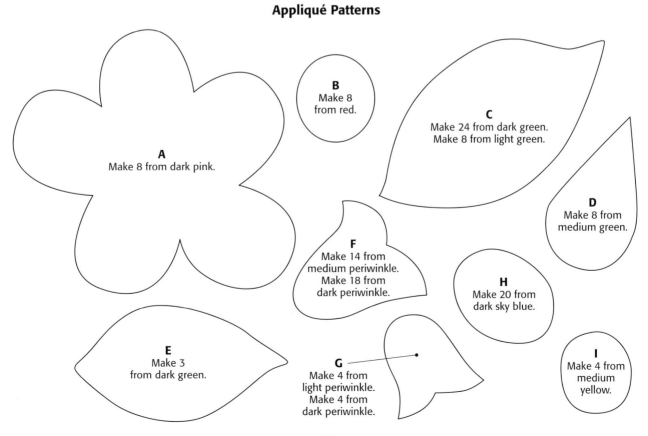

A
Make 8 from dark pink.

B
Make 8
from red.

C
Make 24 from dark green.
Make 8 from light green.

D
Make 8 from
medium green.

F
Make 14 from
medium periwinkle.
Make 18 from
dark periwinkle.

H
Make 20 from
dark sky blue.

E
Make 3
from dark green.

G
Make 4 from
light periwinkle.
Make 4 from
dark periwinkle.

I
Make 4 from
medium
yellow.

Mama's Pop Beads

By Mary Hickey. Quilted by Dawn Kelly.

I first saw this design on an antique quilt at a conference in Columbia, South Carolina, done in an array of 1930s-style scraps. While I absolutely loved it, there was something about it that bothered me. I couldn't figure it out at the time, but later when I saw a picture of it, I realized that it needed a space between the rows of blocks to better define them. With the addition of a plain vertical sashing strip, you don't have to match the block seams between the rows. Of course that makes the sewing easier, and we're always in favor of that!

Finished quilt size: 68½" x 92½"
Finished block size: 6" x 6"

Materials

Yardages are based on 42"-wide fabrics.

- 5 yards *total* of assorted blue fabrics for blocks and outer border
- 1¼ yards *each* of 3 different white fabrics for block backgrounds and vertical sashing strips
- ½ yard of red fabric for inner border
- ¼ yard *each* of bright yellow, pink, purple, green, and red fabric for Diamond blocks
- 5¾ yards of fabric for backing
- 1 yard of fabric for binding
- 72" x 96" piece of batting

Cutting

All measurements include ¼"-wide seam allowances.

From the assorted blue fabrics, cut a *total* of:
30 strips, 2" x 42"
364 squares, 2" x 2"
88 rectangles, 3½" x 6½"
8 rectangles, 1½" x 6½"
4 squares, 6½" x 6½"

From *each* of two of the assorted white fabrics, cut:
6 strips, 2" x 42"

From the remaining white fabric, cut:
4 strips, 2" x 42"

From the remainder of the three assorted white fabrics, cut a *total* of:
92 rectangles, 2" x 6½"
184 squares, 2" x 2"
45 rectangles, 3½" x 6½"

From the bright yellow fabric, cut:
6 squares, 3½" x 3½"

From *each* of the bright pink and purple fabrics, cut:
9 squares, 3½" x 3½"

From *each* of the bright green and red fabrics, cut:
11 squares, 3½" x 3½"

From the red inner-border fabric, cut:
8 strips, 1½" x 42"

From the binding fabric, cut:
332" of 2¼"-wide bias strips

Assembling the Oval Blocks

1. Using a pencil and your rotary-cutting ruler, draw a diagonal line from corner to corner on the wrong side of each of the 2" blue squares. You will use 180 for the Oval blocks; set the remainder aside for the Diamond blocks. With right sides together, place a marked square on opposite corners of each 3½" x 6½" white rectangle as shown. Be sure the lines are oriented in the correct direction. Stitch on the marked lines. Trim ¼" from the stitching line. Flip open the triangles and press the seams toward the blue triangles. Repeat on the opposite corners of each rectangle, orienting the lines in the opposite direction as shown.

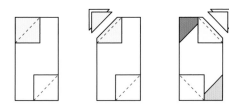

Make 45.

2. Stitch four 2" x 42" assorted blue strips together along the long edges to make a strip set. Make five. Crosscut the strip sets into 90 segments, 2" wide.

Make 5 strip sets.
Cut 90 segments.

3. Using segments from two different strip sets, stitch a segment to the sides of the units from step 1 to complete the Oval blocks.

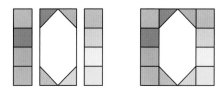

Make 45.

Assembling the Diamond Blocks

1. Draw a diagonal line from corner to corner on the wrong side of each 2" white square. Place two marked squares on opposite corners of each 3½" bright yellow, pink, purple, green, and red square as shown. Be sure the lines are oriented in the direction shown. Stitch on the marked lines. Trim ¼" from the stitching line. Flip open the triangles and press the seams toward the darker color. Repeat on the opposite corners of each square, orienting the lines in the opposite direction as shown.

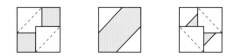

Make 46.

2. Stitch two 2" x 42" blue strips together along one long side to make a strip set. Make five. Crosscut the strip sets into 92 segments, 2" wide.

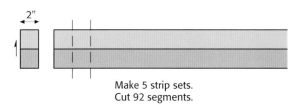

Make 5 strip sets.
Cut 92 segments.

29

3. Stitch a segment from step 2 to the top and bottom of each unit from step 1.

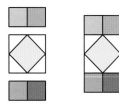

4. Using the 2" blue squares you set aside in step 1 of "Assembling the Oval Blocks," place a marked square on each end of each of the 2" x 6½" white rectangles as shown, right sides together. Be sure the lines are oriented in the directions shown. Stitch on the marked lines. Trim ¼" from the stitching line. Flip open the triangles and press the seams toward the blue triangles.

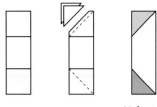

Make 92.

5. Stitch a unit from step 4 to each side of a unit from step 3 as shown to complete the Diamond blocks.

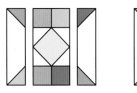

Make 46.

Assembling the Quilt Top

1. Refer to the quilt assembly diagram on page 31 to arrange the blocks in seven vertical rows of 13 blocks each, alternating the Diamond and Oval blocks in each row and from row to row. Stitch the blocks in each row together. Press the seams toward the Oval blocks. In order for the outer pieced border to fit, the rows should measure 78½" long.

2. Stitch two matching 2" x 42" white strips together to make one long strip. Repeat to make a total of eight vertical sashing strips. Trim each sashing strip to 78½".

3. Arrange the sashing strips and block rows. Stitch the rows together.

4. Refer to "Borders with Straight-Sewn Corners" on page 8 to piece the red inner-border strips together. From the pieced strip, cut two strips 78 1/2" long and stitch them to the sides of the quilt top. Press the seams toward the border strips. From the remainder of the pieced strip, cut two strips 56½" long and stitch them to the top and bottom edges of the quilt top. Press the seams toward the border strips.

5. To make the pieced outer side borders, stitch 26 blue 3½" x 6½" rectangles together along the long edges. Make two. Stitch a blue 1½" x 6½" rectangle to each end of each strip. Stitch the strips to the sides of the quilt top.

6. To make the pieced outer top and bottom borders, stitch 18 blue 3½" x 6½" rectangles together along the long edges. Make two. Stitch a blue 1½" x 6½" rectangle to each end of each strip. Add a blue 6½" square to each end of each strip. Stitch the strips to the top and bottom edges of the quilt top.

Finishing the Quilt

Refer to "Quiltmaking Techniques" on page 5 for details on quilt finishing, if needed.

1. Cut and piece the backing fabric so it is approximately 4" to 6" larger than the quilt top.

2. Layer the backing, batting, and quilt top; baste the layers together.

3. Hand or machine quilt as desired. The quilt shown was machine quilted with vines, loops, flowers, leaves, and daisies.

4. Trim the batting and backing fabric even with the quilt top. Make a hanging sleeve and attach it to the quilt back.

5. Bind the quilt edges with the bias strips. Add a label to the quilt back.

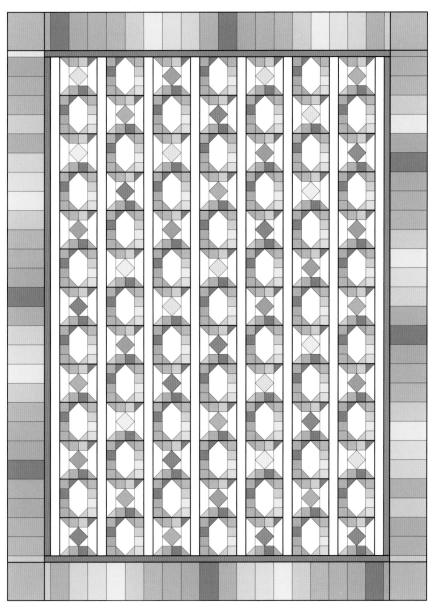

Quilt Assembly

Helen's Wreaths

By Mary Hickey. Quilted by Fannie Schwartz.

In this quilt, a soft wash of peaches, pale greens, and beiges are used to create the Stepping Stone blocks that provide the background for four lovely, button-embellished appliquéd wreaths. The blocks that form the frame around each wreath are made of a combination of light and dark green fabric, while the block in the center of each wreath is made from all light green fabrics. Although I use the terms light and dark, the fabrics have very little contrast with each other, so be sure to use many different prints. This will create interesting details that catch your eye and keep the quilt from looking flat and one-dimensional.

Finished quilt size: 100" x 100"
Finished block size: 9" x 9"

Materials

Yardages are based on 42"-wide fabrics.

- 3¼ yards of large-scale floral for outer border
- 2⅝ yards of cream tone-on-tone for blocks and setting triangles
- 2⅛ yards of cream fabric #3 for alternate blocks
- 1⅛ yards *each* of cream fabrics #1 and #2 for blocks
- ⅞ yard of light green fabric for blocks and leaf appliqués
- ¾ yard of dark green fabric #1 for blocks and leaf appliqués
- ⅝ yard of dark green fabric #2 for blocks
- ⅝ yard of peach fabric for flower appliqués and inner border
- Scraps of assorted peach and rust fabrics for flower appliqués
- 9 yards of fabric for backing
- 1 yard of fabric for binding
- 104" x 104" piece of batting
- 1½ yards of paper-backed fusible web for fusible-web appliqué **OR** lightweight cotton or interfacing for face-and-turn appliqué
- 20 assorted peach and rust ⅝"- to ¾"-diameter buttons for centers of flower appliqués

Cutting

All measurements include ¼"-wide seam allowances.

From the cream tone-on-tone, cut:
17 strips, 2" x 42"
2 strips, 3½" x 42"; crosscut into:
    2 strips, 3½" x 21"
    8 squares, 3½" x 3½"
3 strips, 14" x 42"; crosscut into 5 squares, 14" x 14". Cut each square in half twice diagonally to yield 20 side setting triangles.
2 squares, 7½" x 7½"; cut each square in half once diagonally to yield 4 corner setting triangles

From the light green fabric, cut:
9 strips, 2" x 42"
1 strip, 3½" x 21"

From *each* of the cream fabrics #1 and #2, cut:
7 strips, 3½" x 42"; crosscut 3 into 32 squares,
  3½" x 3½"

From *each* of the dark green fabrics #1 and #2, cut:
4 strips, 2" x 42"

2 strips, 3½" x 42"

From the cream fabric #3, cut:
7 strips, 9½" x 42"; crosscut into 25 squares,
  9½" x 9½"

From the peach fabric, cut:
9 strips, 2" x 42"

From the *lengthwise* grain of the large-scale floral, cut:
2 strips, 10" x 85"

2 strips, 10" x 105"

From the binding fabric, cut:
410" of 2¼"-wide bias strips

Assembling the Stepping Stone Blocks

1. Sew a 2" x 42" cream tone-on-tone strip to one long side of each 2" x 42" light green, dark green #1, and dark green #2 strip to make strip sets. Make the number of strip sets indicated for each color combination. Crosscut the strip sets into the number of 2"-wide segments indicated.

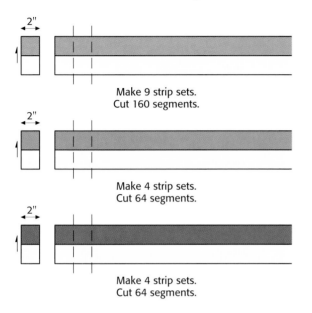

Make 9 strip sets.
Cut 160 segments.

Make 4 strip sets.
Cut 64 segments.

Make 4 strip sets.
Cut 64 segments.

2. Stitch two matching segments together as shown to make a four-patch unit. Make the number of four-patch units indicated for each color combination.

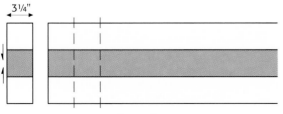

Make 80.   Make 32.   Make 32.

3. Sew a 3½" x 21" cream tone-on-tone strip to both long sides of the 3½" x 21" light green strip to make a strip set. Crosscut the strip set into four segments, 3½" wide.

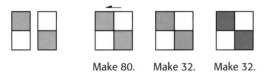

Make 1 strip set.
Cut 4 segments.

4. Sew a cream #1 strip to each long side of each 3½" x 42" dark green #1 strip. Sew a cream #2 strip to each long side of each 3½" x 42" dark green #2 strip. Make two strip sets with each dark green print. Cut the strip sets from each dark green color combination into 16 segments, 3½" wide (32 total).

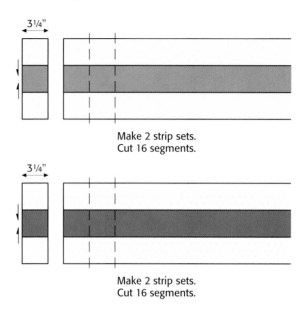

Make 2 strip sets.
Cut 16 segments.

Make 2 strip sets.
Cut 16 segments.

5. Stitch the four-patch units; the segments from steps 3 and 4; and the 3½" cream tone-on-tone, cream #1, and cream #2 squares together as shown to make block variations A, B, and C. Be sure to use the same 3½" cream square in each block that was used in the strip set. Make the number of blocks indicated for each variation.

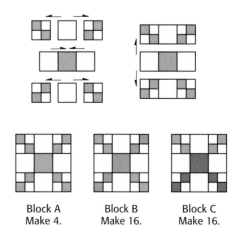

Block A
Make 4.

Block B
Make 16.

Block C
Make 16.

Assembling the Quilt Top

1. Arrange the Stepping Stone blocks, the 9½" cream #3 squares, and the side and corner setting triangles into four quadrants of diagonal rows as shown. Stitch the pieces in each row of each quadrant together. Press the seams toward the Stepping Stone blocks. Do not sew the quadrants together at this time.

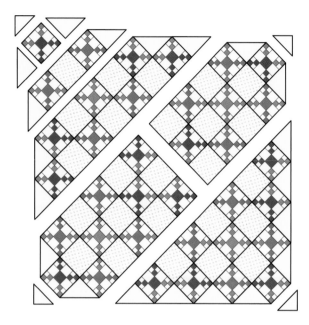

2. Refer to "Appliqué Methods" on page 6 to make the appliqué shapes and apply them to the blocks in each quadrant, using patterns A–C on page 37 and the desired appliqué method. Refer to the quilt assembly diagram and the photo on page 34 for placement as needed. Notice that the appliqué wreaths are sewn almost entirely on the cream print #3 squares; only the tips of the leaves overlap onto the Stepping Stone blocks.

3. Stitch the quadrants together.

4. Refer to "Borders with Straight-Sewn Corners" on page 8 to join and trim the peach strips to the correct lengths and stitch them to the quilt top. Press the seams toward the border strips. Measure the quilt for outer

borders in the same manner. Cut the floral strips to the correct lengths and add them to the quilt top. Press the seams toward the peach border strips.

Quilt Assembly

Finishing the Quilt

Refer to "Quiltmaking Techniques" on page 5 for details on quilt finishing, if needed.

1. Cut and piece the backing fabric so it is approximately 4" to 6" larger than the quilt top.

2. Layer the backing, batting, and quilt top; baste the layers together.

3. Hand or machine quilt as desired. The quilt shown was quilted with grids and outline quilting.

4. Attach the buttons to the centers of the flower appliqués.

5. Trim the batting and backing fabric even with the quilt top. Make a hanging sleeve and attach it to the quilt back.

6. Bind the quilt edges with the bias strips. Add a label to the quilt back.

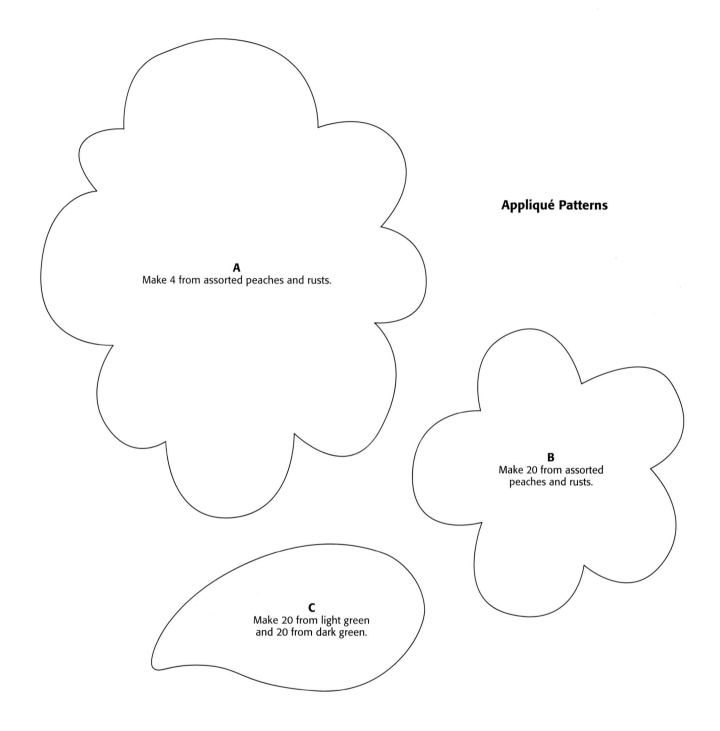

Appliqué Patterns

A
Make 4 from assorted peaches and rusts.

B
Make 20 from assorted
peaches and rusts.

C
Make 20 from light green
and 20 from dark green.

Beach Music

By Mary Hickey. Quilted by Dawn Kelly.

Fresh blue and yellow rays bounce from a washed white background in this bright and cheerful quilt. Two block designs combine to make a swinging rhythm along the rows of triangles. The backgrounds of the Double Snowball blocks link with beams of light in the Star blocks, sending a third beat dancing around the blocks.

Finished quilt size: 91" x 91"
Finished block size: 10" x 10"

Materials

Yardages are based on 42"-wide fabrics.

- 3 yards *total* of assorted white fabrics for Star blocks
- 3 yards *total* of assorted medium blue fabrics for blocks
- 3 yards of blue floral for outer border
- 2⅝ yards of white fabric for Double Snowball blocks
- ¾ yard *total* of assorted dark blue fabrics for blocks
- ¾ yard *total* of assorted yellow fabrics for blocks
- ¾ yard of dark blue fabric for inner border
- ⅝ yard of yellow fabric for middle border
- 8½ yards of fabric for backing
- ¾ yard of fabric for binding
- 95" x 95" piece of batting

Cutting

All measurements include ¼"-wide seam allowances.

From the assorted dark blue fabrics, cut:
8 strips, 2½" x 42"

From the assorted white fabrics, cut:
22 strips, 2½" x 42"; crosscut 7 into 100 squares, 2½" x 2½"

3 strips, 12½" x 42"; crosscut into 8 squares, 12½" x 12½"

From the assorted yellow fabrics, cut:
9 strips, 2½" x 42"; crosscut 7 into 96 squares, 2½" x 2½"

From the assorted medium blue fabrics, cut:
3 strips, 12½" x 42"; crosscut into 8 squares, 12½" x 12½"

12 strips, 4½" x 42"; crosscut into 24 sets of 4 squares, 4½" x 4½" (96 total)

From the white fabric for the Double Snowball blocks, cut:
8 strips, 10½" x 42"; crosscut into 24 squares, 10½" x 10½"

From the dark blue inner-border fabric, cut:
8 strips, 2¼" x 42"

From the yellow middle-border fabric, cut:
10 strips, 1½" x 42"

From the *lengthwise* grain of the blue floral, cut:
2 strips, 9" x 78"

2 strips, 9" x 95"

From the binding fabric, cut:
382" of 2¼"-wide bias strips

Assembling the Star Blocks

1. Sew a 2½" x 42" assorted dark blue strip to both long sides of a 2½" x 42" assorted white strip to make strip set A. Make four. Crosscut the strip sets into 50 segments, 2½" wide.

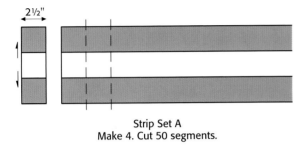

Strip Set A
Make 4. Cut 50 segments.

2. Sew a 2½" x 42" assorted white strip to both long sides of a 2½" x 42" assorted yellow strip to make strip set B. Make two. Crosscut the strip sets into 25 segments, 2½" wide.

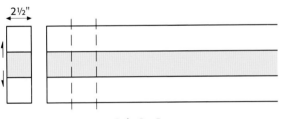

Strip Set B
Make 2. Cut 25 segments.

3. Arrange two strip set A segments and one strip set B segment as shown. Sew the segments together to make a nine-patch unit. Make 25.

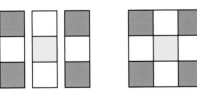

Make 25.

4. Refer to "Half-Square-Triangle Units" on page 5 to make the half-square triangles. Pair each 12½" medium blue square with a 12½" assorted white square. Cut the strips 2½" wide. Cut 200 half-square triangles.

5. With right sides together, lay the half-square triangles on the seven remaining 2½" x 42" assorted white strips, placing the squares side by side as shown with just a slight amount of space between them. Stitch along the long edge as shown. Press the seams toward the white strips. Place your ruler on the strip so it spans the white strip and the half-square triangle. Align your rotary-cutting ruler with the right edge of the half-square triangle and cut across the strip. Trim the left side of each segment even with the half-square triangle.

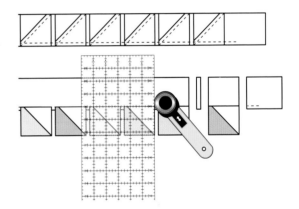

6. Stitch the remaining half-square triangles to the top of each segment from step 5 as shown.

7. Stitch a segment from step 6 to the top and bottom of each nine-patch unit. Stitch a 2½" assorted white square to the top and bottom of

each of the remaining segments, and then stitch these units to the sides of the nine-patch unit to complete the Star blocks.

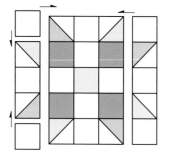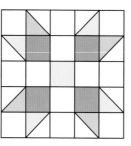

Make 25.

Assembling the Double Snowball Blocks

1. Using a pencil and your rotary-cutting ruler, draw a diagonal line from corner to corner on the wrong side of each 4½" medium blue square. Draw a second line ½" from the first line.

½"

2. With right sides together, place a marked square in one corner of each 10½" white square as shown. Stitch along both sets of marked lines. Repeat for the remaining corners of each square. Align the ¼" line of your rotary-cutting ruler along the first seam line of each square and trim away the excess fabric. Flip open the triangles on the large square and press toward the blue triangles.

Note: Because the blue squares on the corners of the Double Snowball blocks are so large, I suggest sewing a second seam ½" from the first seam, toward the outer corner of the block. Once you have trimmed the outer triangles away, you will have 100 extra half-square triangles, each measuring 3½", for a later quilt. What a bonus!

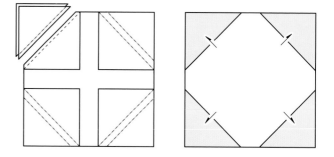

3. Draw a diagonal line from corner to corner on the wrong side of each 2½" assorted yellow square. Place a marked square on each corner of the squares from step 2. Stitch on the marked lines. Trim ¼" from the stitching line. Flip open the triangles and press the seams toward the yellow triangles to complete the Double Snowball blocks.

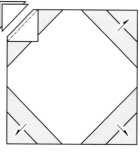

Make 24.

Assembling the Quilt Top

1. Refer to the quilt assembly diagram to arrange the blocks into seven horizontal rows of seven blocks each, alternating the Star and Double Snowball blocks in each row and from row to row as shown.

2. Stitch the blocks in each row together; press the seams toward the Double Snowball blocks. Stitch the rows together; press the seams in one direction.

3. Refer to "Borders with Straight-Sewn Corners" on page 8 to piece and cut the 2¼"-wide dark blue strips to the correct lengths and stitch them to the quilt top for the inner border.

4. The middle borders are pinned in place and then stitched down when the outer borders are added. For the middle border, stitch the 1½" x 42" yellow middle-border strips together end to end. Press the yellow strip in half lengthwise, wrong sides together. Measure the length of the quilt top through the center. From both the yellow strips and blue floral strips, cut two strips to the correct length for the side borders. Pin the yellow strips to the sides of the quilt top, aligning the raw edges. Do not pin the blue strips in place yet. Measure the width of the quilt top through the center and cut two yellow strips to the correct length. Pin these strips to the top and bottom edges of the quilt top. Next, measure the quilt top for the outer side borders and trim the blue floral 9" x 78" strips to the correct length. Pin the strips to the sides of the quilt top, placing them over the yellow strips, raw edges aligned; stitch. Press the seams toward the quilt top. Measure the width of the quilt top through the center. Trim the blue floral 9" x 95" strips to the correct length and sew them to the top and bottom edges of the quilt top. Press the seams toward the quilt top.

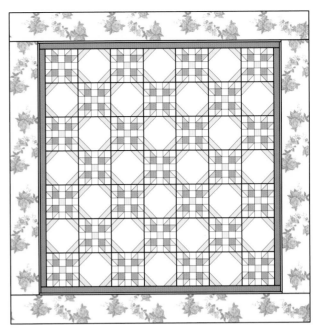

Quilt Assembly

Finishing the Quilt

Refer to "Quiltmaking Techniques" on page 5 for details on quilt finishing, if needed.

1. Cut and piece the backing fabric so it is approximately 4" to 6" larger than the quilt top.

2. Layer the backing, batting, and quilt top; baste the layers together.

3. Hand or machine quilt as desired. The quilt shown was machine quilted with large flowers in the centers of the Double Snowball blocks, in-the-ditch quilting in the rest of the blocks, and a feathered design in the borders.

4. Trim the batting and backing fabric even with the quilt top. Make a hanging sleeve and attach it to the quilt back.

5. Bind the quilt edges with the bias strips. Add a label to the quilt back.

Regatta

By Mary Hickey. Quilted by Dawn Kelly.

Quilters have always loved traditional sailboat quilts. This dashing little boat is particularly fun to make because most of it is assembled using quick corners. Traditional quick corners are made using squares. This boat takes the traditional technique a step further, using both squares and rectangles. The little boats are easy to make and great fun to assemble in a quilt. By cutting some of the fabrics facing up and some facing down, we will be able to make half of the boats sail to the east and half sail to the west without having to think about it.

Finished quilt size: 49" x 49"
Finished block size: 7½" x 7½"

Materials

Yardages are based on 42"-wide fabrics.

- 1¾ yards of blue fabric for background
- ¾ yard of red striped fabric for outer border*
- ½ yard *total* of assorted blue striped fabrics for sails
- ⅜ yard *total* of assorted red fabrics for boat hulls and flags
- 3¼ yards of fabric for backing
- ⅞ yard of fabric for binding
- 53" x 53" piece of batting

Stripes must run the length of the fabric to achieve the same results as the featured quilt.

Cutting

All measurements include ¼"-wide seam allowances.

From the blue fabric, cut:
1 strip, 3¼" x 42"; crosscut into 6 rectangles, 3¼" x 6¼"

5 strips, 1" x 42"; crosscut into:
    12 rectangles, 1" x 8"
    12 rectangles, 1" x 5½"

3 strips, 2½" x 42"; crosscut into:
    12 squares, 2½" x 2½"
    24 rectangles, 2½" x 3¼"

2 strips, 3" x 42"; crosscut into:
    12 rectangles, 1½" x 3"
    12 rectangles, 3" x 4½"

3 strips, 8" x 42"; crosscut into 13 squares, 8" x 8"

4 strips, 2" x 42"

From the assorted blue striped fabrics, cut:
12 rectangles, 5" x 5½"
12 squares, 3" x 3"

From the assorted red prints, cut:
12 squares, 1½" x 1½"
12 rectangles, 2½" x 6¾"

From the red striped fabric, cut:
5 strips, 4½" x 42"

From the binding fabric, cut:
206" of 2¼"-wide bias strips

Assembling the Sailboat Blocks

1. To make the large sail units, place the 3¼" x 6¼" blue rectangles on your cutting mat so that three are right side up and three are wrong side up. Cut each rectangle in half diagonally, making all of the cuts in the same direction.

2. Place the 5" x 5½" blue striped rectangles on your cutting mat so that six are right side up and six are wrong side up. On each rectangle, measure 2¾" from the upper-left edge and make a mark. Cut from the mark to the lower-left corner of each rectangle.

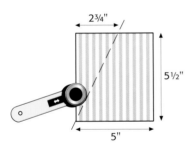

3. Stitch the blue triangles to the cut side of the blue striped rectangles as shown. Make six units with the blue triangle on the left side and six units with the blue triangle on the right side. Press the seams toward the blue triangles.

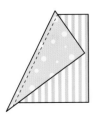 

Make 6.   Make 6.

4. Using a pencil, draw a diagonal line from corner to corner on the wrong side of each 2½" blue square. Place a marked square on each unit from step 3, positioning it on the side opposite the large blue triangle. Stitch on the marked lines. Trim ¼" from the stitching lines. Press the seams toward the small blue triangles.

5. To make the flag units, draw a diagonal line from corner to corner on the wrong side of each 1½" red square. Place a marked square on the left end of six 1½" x 3" blue rectangles as shown. Place the remaining marked squares on the right end of the remaining 1½" x 3" blue rectangles as shown. Be sure the squares are placed on the rectangles so the lines are running in the correct directions. Stitch on the marked lines. Trim ¼" from the stitching lines. Press the seams toward the blue rectangles.

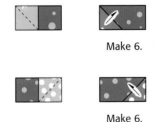

Make 6.

Make 6.

6. To make the small sail units, draw a diagonal line from corner to corner on the wrong side of each 3" blue striped square. Place a marked square on the end of six 3" x 4½" blue rectangles as shown. Place the remaining marked squares on the remaining blue rectangles as shown. Be sure the squares are placed on the rectangles so the lines are running in the

47

correct directions. Stitch on the marked lines. Trim ¼" from the stitching lines. Press the seam toward the blue striped fabric.

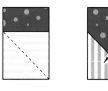

Make 6.

Make 6.

7. Stitch a 1" x 5½" blue rectangle to each large sail unit on the side with the small blue triangle as shown. Stitch a flag unit to the top of each small sail unit so that the flag and sail are pointing in the same direction. Stitch the large and small sail units together so you have six boats sailing east and six sailing west.

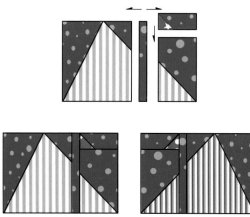

Make 6.   Make 6.

8. To make the hull units, place a 2½" x 3¼" blue rectangle on the ends of each 2½" x 6¾" red rectangle, right sides together, as shown. Draw a diagonal line on the wrong side of the

red rectangle as shown. Stitch on the marked lines. Trim ¼" from the stitching line. Press the seams toward the blue rectangles.

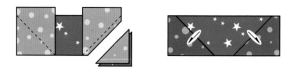

9. Sew a 1" x 8" blue rectangle to the top of each hull unit.

10. Stitch a hull unit to each sail unit to complete the Sailboat blocks.

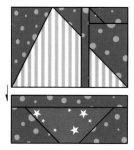

 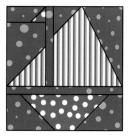

Make 6.   Make 6.

48

Assembling the Quilt Top

1. Refer to the quilt assembly diagram to arrange the blocks and 8" blue squares into five horizontal rows of five blocks each, alternating the blocks and squares in each row and from row to row as shown.

2. Stitch the blocks in each row together; press the seams toward the Sailboat blocks. Stitch the rows together; press the seams in one direction.

3. Refer to "Borders with Straight-Sewn Corners" on page 8 to trim the 2" x 42" blue strips to the correct lengths and stitch them to the quilt top. Press the seams toward the borders.

4. Refer to "Borders with Mitered Corners" on page 9 to piece and cut the red striped strips to the correct lengths and stitch them to the quilt top, mitering the corners.

Finishing the Quilt

Refer to "Quiltmaking Techniques" on page 5 for details on quilt finishing, if needed.

1. Cut and piece the backing fabric so it is approximately 4" to 6" larger than the quilt top.

2. Layer the backing, batting, and quilt top; baste the layers together.

3. Hand or machine quilt as desired. The quilt shown was machine quilted with waves and outline quilting in the water and around the boats, and large and small loops in the striped border.

4. Trim the batting and backing fabric even with the quilt top. Make a hanging sleeve and attach it to the quilt back.

5. Bind the quilt edges with the bias strips. Add a label to the quilt back.

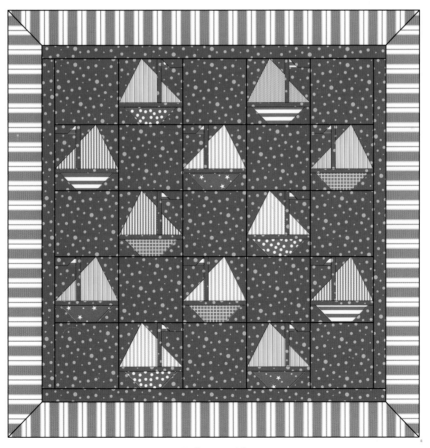

Quilt Assembly

Wind Fluttering over the Sea

By Mary Hickey. Quilted by Dawn Kelly.

This is a scrappy quilt with a cool color scheme of sky blues, periwinkle blues, aqua blues, and sea greens. If you have a substantial fabric collection, you are all set. All you have to do is gather a set of lights and a set of darks or mediums in these colors. If you're going to buy fabrics, I suggest buying a group of fat quarters. They will give you the most efficient use of your fabrics.

Finished quilt size: 49½" x 49½"
Finished block size: 8" x 8"

Materials

Yardages are based on 42"-wide fabrics.

- 1¾ yards of multicolored print for outer border
- ⅝ yard *total* of assorted light sky blue fabrics for blocks
- ⅝ yard *total* of assorted medium and/or dark sky blue fabrics for blocks
- ½ yard *total* of assorted light aqua fabrics for blocks
- ½ yard *total* of assorted medium and/or dark aqua fabrics for blocks
- ½ yard *total* of assorted light periwinkle fabrics for blocks
- ½ yard *total* of assorted medium and/or dark periwinkle fabrics for blocks
- ½ yard *total* of assorted light green fabrics for blocks
- ½ yard *total* of assorted medium and/or dark green fabrics for blocks
- ½ yard of dark periwinkle fabric for inner border
- 3¼ yards of fabric for backing
- ⅞ yard of fabric for binding
- 53" x 53" piece of batting

Cutting

All measurements include ¼"-wide seam allowances.

From the light sky blue fabrics, cut a *total* of:
5 squares, 9" x 9"
7 squares, 4½" x 4½"

From the medium and/or dark sky blue fabrics, cut a *total* of:
5 squares, 9" x 9"
7 squares, 4½" x 4½"

From the assorted light aqua fabrics, cut a *total* of:
4 squares, 9" x 9"
6 squares, 4½" x 4½"

From the assorted medium and/or dark aqua fabrics, cut a *total* of:
4 squares, 9" x 9"
6 squares, 4½" x 4½"

From the assorted light periwinkle fabrics, cut a *total* of:
4 squares, 9" x 9"
6 squares, 4½" x 4½"

From the assorted medium and/or dark periwinkle fabrics, cut a *total* of:
4 squares, 9" x 9"
6 squares, 4½" x 4½"

From the assorted light green fabrics, cut a *total* of:

4 squares, 9" x 9"

6 squares, 4½" x 4½"

From the assorted medium and/or dark green fabrics, cut a *total* of:

4 squares, 9" x 9"

6 squares, 4½" x 4½"

From the dark periwinkle inner-border fabric, cut:

5 strips, 1¾" x 42"

From the *lengthwise* grain of the multicolored print, cut:

4 strips, 3¾" x 54"

From the binding fabric, cut:

208" of 2¼"-wide bias strips

Assembling the Blocks

1. Using the 9" squares of the assorted fabrics, refer to "Half-Square-Triangle Units" on page 5 to make the half-square triangles. Pair each light square with a medium or dark square from the same color family. Cut the strips 2½" wide. Cut the number of 2½" squares indicated for each color combination.

Cut 56. Cut 48. Cut 48. Cut 48.

2. Stitch four half-square triangles from the same color family together as shown.

3. Arrange two half-square-triangle units from the same color family and a 4½" light and medium or dark square from the same color family as the half-square-triangle units into two rows as shown. Stitch the units in each row together,

and then stitch the rows together to complete the blocks. Make 25.

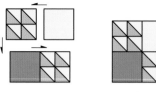

Make 25.

Assembling the Quilt Top

1. Refer to the photograph on page 50 to arrange the blocks into five horizontal rows of five blocks each, rotating the blocks to create the design.

2. Sew the blocks in each row together; press the seams in one direction, alternating the direction from row to row. Sew the rows together; press the seams in one direction.

3. Refer to "Borders with Mitered Corners" on page 9 to piece and cut the dark periwinkle inner-border strips to the correct lengths. Piece them together with the multicolored outer-border strips to form a border unit. Stitch the units to the quilt top and miter the corners. Press the seams toward the periwinkle strips.

Finishing the Quilt

Refer to "Quiltmaking Techniques" on page 5 for details on quilt finishing, if needed.

1. Cut and piece the backing fabric so it is approximately 4" to 6" larger than the quilt top.

2. Layer the backing, batting, and quilt top; baste the layers together.

3. Hand or machine quilt as desired. The quilt shown was machine quilted with beautiful waves and swirls to create the feeling of wind over water.

4. Trim the batting and backing even with the quilt top. Make a hanging sleeve and attach it to the quilt back.

5. Bind the quilt edges with the bias strips. Add a label to the quilt back.

There's a Whale in the Bay

By Mary Hickey. Quilted by Dawn Kelly.

We live on a beautiful little bay on Puget Sound in Washington State. Whales do not normally swim into a bay as small as ours, but on one cold, rainy day in 2000, our neighbors called in a state of great excitement to tell us to hurry onto our deck because there was a whale in the bay swimming toward our house. We ran out just in time to see a huge gray whale rise out of the water and give a rousing spout into the wind and rain. The deep sound of its exhalation and the sheer size of the whale shook our knees and took our breath away. To commemorate the day, my husband wrote a rhyme, which I spell out in this quilt using nautical signal flags (used in ship-to-ship communication):

A mighty whale, bold and gray
Visited us in Liberty Bay

The flags for this quilt measure just 4" x 6". I've included instructions for every letter of the alphabet, so don't hesitate to make up a little message of your own and send it to someone you love.

Finished quilt size: 81" x 81"
Finished block size: 6" x 7½"

Materials
Yardages are based on 42"-wide fabrics.

- 3⅞ yards of light blue fabric for background and first and third borders
- 2¾ yards of royal blue fabric for blocks and fourth border
- 1¼ yards of white fabric for blocks and striped second border
- 1¼ yards of red fabric for blocks and striped second border
- ½ yard of yellow fabric for blocks
- 5 yards of fabric for backing
- 1 yard of fabric for binding
- 85" x 85" piece of batting

Note: I have adapted some of the flags to make the piecing easier and substituted blue for the black normally used in the flags. It is very important to hang the flags right side up, so double-check your blocks with the chart before you set them into the quilt.

Cutting

To make the featured quilt, cut the following pieces and then refer to "Piecing the Flags" to cut the pieces required for each letter. All measurements include ¼"-wide seam allowances.

From the light blue fabric, cut:

7 strips, 6½" x 42"; crosscut into:

    44 rectangles, 4" x 6½"

    3 rectangles, 1" x 6½"

    9 rectangles, 6½" x 8"

1 strip, 4½" x 42"; crosscut into:

    3 rectangles, 3½" x 4½"

    3 rectangles, 3" x 4½"

    3 rectangles, 1" x 4½"

6 rectangles, 2" x 2½"

10 strips, 3" x 42"

4 strips, 4" x 42"

2 strips, 4½" x 42"

8 strips, 2½" x 42"

From the white fabric, cut:

3 squares, 3" x 3"

3 squares, 3½" x 3½"

5 strips, 2½" x 42"

From the red fabric, cut:

1 rectangle, 2" x 5½"

5 strips, 2½" x 42"

From the royal blue fabric, cut:

2 rectangles, 2" x 5½"

8 strips, 4¾" x 42"

From the binding fabric, cut:

334" of 2¼"-wide bias strips

Piecing the Flags

Cutting instructions are given for the entire flag alphabet, but you need only some of the "letters" to make the quilt shown on page 55. After a letter, the number in parentheses indicates how many of that letter to make for the featured quilt. After cutting dimensions, the number in parentheses shows how many pieces to cut for each letter.

Letter	White	Red	Royal Blue	Yellow
A (5)	2½" x 4½" (2)		2½" x 4½" 2½" x 2½" (2)	
B (3)	2½" x 4½"	4½" x 4½" 2½" x 2½" (2)		
C	1" x 6½" (2)	1½" x 6½"	1½" x 6½" (2)	
D (3)			2½" x 6½"	1½" x 6½" (2)
E (3)		2½" x 6½"	2½" x 6½"	
F	See templates on page 61.			
G (2)			1½" x 4½" (3)	1½" x 4½" (3)
H (2)	3½" x 4½"	3½" x 4½"		
I (5)			3¼"-diameter (finished) circle	4½" x 6½"
J	2" x 6½"		1¾" x 6½" (2)	
K			3½" x 4½"	3½" x 4½"
L (3)			2½" x 3½" (2)	2½" x 3½" (2)
M (1)	See templates on page 62.			
N (2)	1½" x 8" (2)		1½" x 8" (2)	
O (1)		5" x 7"		5" x 7"
P	2" x 4"		1¾" x 4" (2) 1¾" x 4½" (2)	
Q				4½" x 6½"
R (2)		2¾" x 4½" (2)		2" x 4½" 2" x 6½"
S (2)	1¾" x 4" (2) 1¾" x 4½" (2)		2" x 4"	
T (3)	2½" x 4½"	2½" x 4½"	2½" x 4½"	
U (1)	2½" x 3½" (2)	2½" x 3½" (2)		
V (1)	See templates on page 62.			
W (1)	1¼" x 3½" (2) 1¼" x 3" (2)	1½" x 3½"	1¼" x 4½" (2) 1¼" x 5" (2)	
X	2¾" x 4½"		2" x 4½" 2" x 6½"	
Y (4)		6" x 9"		6" x 9"
Z	See templates on page 63.			

Flag Assembly

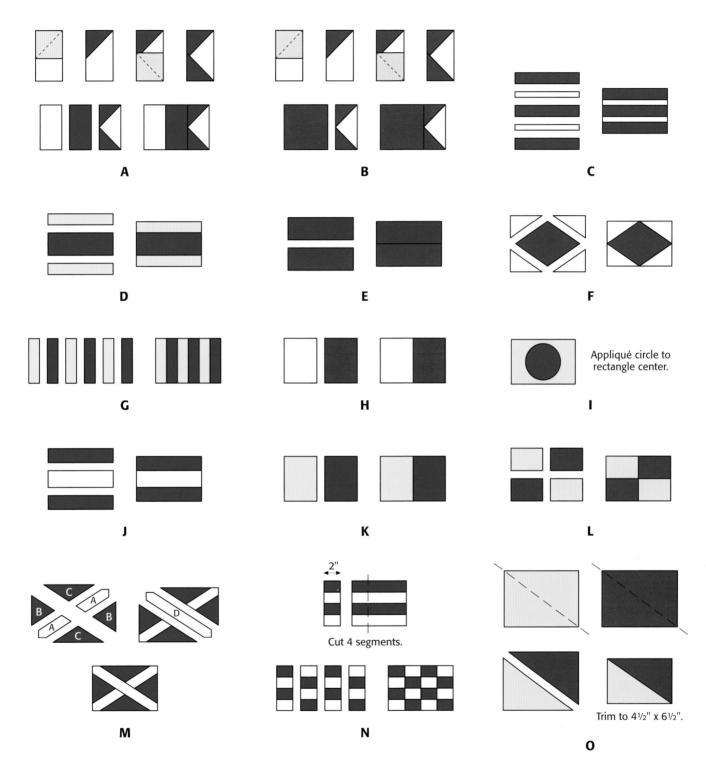

Appliqué circle to rectangle center.

2"

Cut 4 segments.

Trim to 4½" x 6½".

Flag Assembly

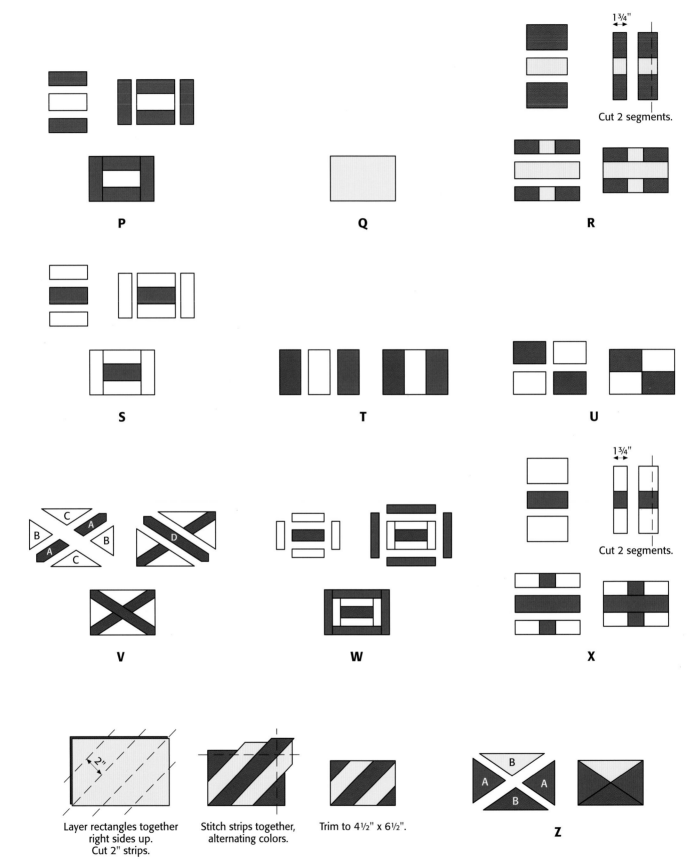

Assembling the Flag Blocks

1. Refer to "Piecing the Flags" and "Flag Assembly" to make the number of flags needed for each letter.

2. Stitch a 4" x 6½" light blue rectangle to the top of each flag.

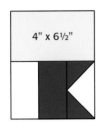

Assembling the Sailboat Blocks

1. To make the sail units, draw a diagonal line from corner to corner on the wrong side of each 3" and 3½" white square.

2. With right sides together, place a 3" white square on the lower end of each 3" x 4½" light blue rectangle as shown. Repeat with the 3½" white squares and the 3½" x 4½" light blue rectangles. Be sure the squares are placed on the rectangles so the lines are running in the directions shown. Stitch on the marked lines. Trim ¼" from the stitching lines. Press the seams toward the rectangles.

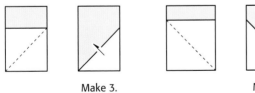

Make 3.   Make 3.

3. Stitch one of each size sail unit and a 1" x 4½" light blue strip together as shown.

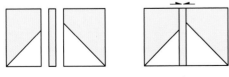

Make 3.

4. To make the hull units, with right sides together, place a 2" x 2½" light blue rectangle on each end of the 2" x 5½" red and royal blue rectangles as shown. Draw a diagonal line on the wrong side of the red and royal blue rectangles as shown. Stitch on the marked lines. Trim ¼" from the stitching line. Press the seams toward the light blue rectangles.

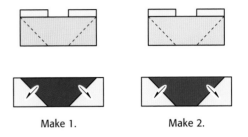

Make 1.   Make 2.

5. Sew a 1" x 6½" light blue rectangle to the top of each hull unit.

6. Stitch a hull unit to each sail unit to complete the Sailboat blocks.

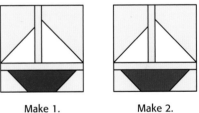

Make 1.   Make 2.

Assembling the Quilt Top

1. Refer to the quilt assembly diagram to arrange the Flag blocks, the Sailboat blocks, and the 6½" x 8" light blue rectangles into seven vertical rows. Be careful to orient the Flag blocks correctly.

2. Stitch the pieces in each row together. Press the seams toward the bottom of the strip.

3. Stitch the 3" x 42" light blue strips together end to end to make one continuous strip. From the strip cut six 60½"-long sashing strips.

4. Alternately stitch the block rows and sashing strips together as shown in the quilt assembly diagram, beginning and ending with a block row. Press the seams toward the strips.

5. Stitch the 4" x 42" light blue strips together end to end. From the strip, cut two strips 60½" long for the inner side borders. Stitch the strips to the sides of the quilt top. Stitch the 4½" x 42" light blue strips together end to end. Trim the pieced strip to 64½" long. Stitch the pieced strip to the bottom of the quilt top. Press the seam toward the pieced strip.

6. To make the pieced second border, stitch a 2½" x 42" red strip to each 2½" x 42" white strip along one long edge. Make five strip sets. Press the seams toward the red strips. Crosscut the strip sets into 66 segments, 2½" wide.

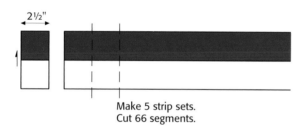

2½"

Make 5 strip sets.
Cut 66 segments.

7. For the pieced side borders, stitch 16 segments together end to end so that the colors alternate between red and white. Make two. Repeat to stitch 17 segments together for the top and bottom borders. Make two. Stitch the side borders to the sides of the quilt top, orienting the strips so a white square is at the top of the left border and a red square is at the top of the right border. Stitch the top and bottom borders to the quilt top and bottom edges, orienting the strips so the square at the ends of each strip is the alternate color of the side border square it meets.

8. Refer to "Borders with Straight-Sewn Corners" on page 8 to piece and cut the 2½" x 42" light blue third border strips to the

correct lengths and stitch them to the quilt top. Press the seams toward the border strips. Repeat with the 4¾" royal blue strips for the fourth border.

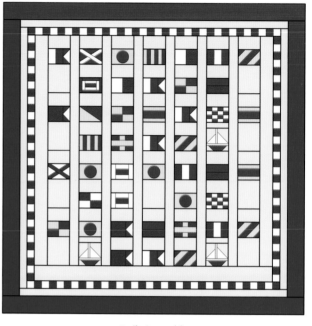

Quilt Assembly

Finishing the Quilt

Refer to "Quiltmaking Techniques" on page 5 for details on quilt finishing, if needed.

1. Cut and piece the backing fabric so it is approximately 4" to 6" larger than the quilt top.

2. Layer the backing, batting, and quilt top; baste the layers together.

3. Hand or machine quilt as desired. The quilt shown was machine quilted with artful anchors, wild waves, jaunty sailboats, and wonderful whales.

4. Trim the batting and backing fabric even with the quilt top. Make a hanging sleeve and attach it to the quilt back.

5. Bind the quilt edges with the bias strips. Add a label to the quilt back.

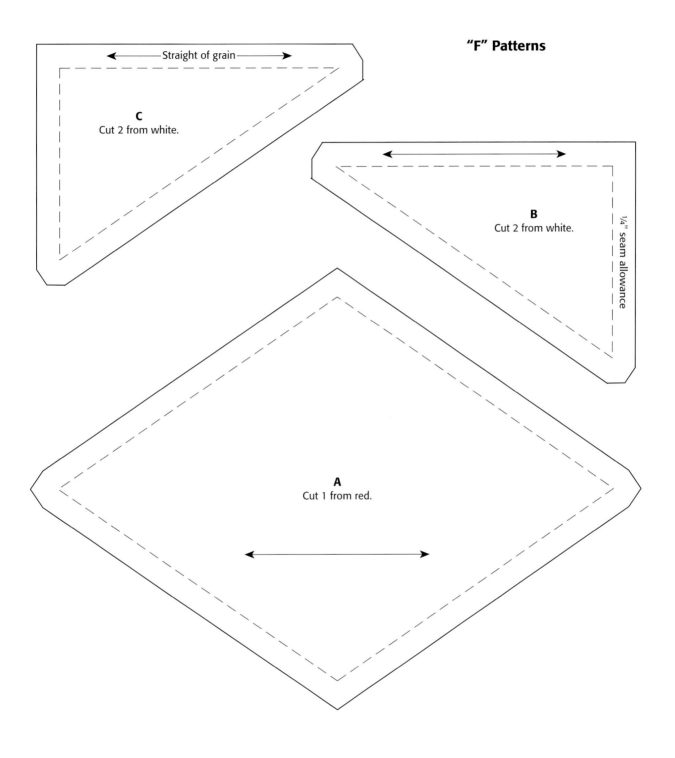

"F" Patterns

"M" and "V" Patterns

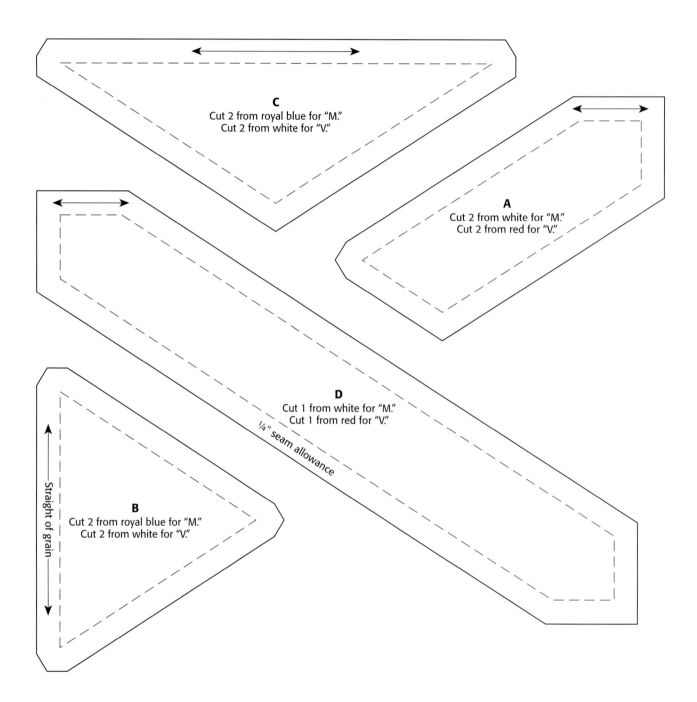

C
Cut 2 from royal blue for "M."
Cut 2 from white for "V."

A
Cut 2 from white for "M."
Cut 2 from red for "V."

D
Cut 1 from white for "M."
Cut 1 from red for "V."

¼" seam allowance

Straight of grain

B
Cut 2 from royal blue for "M."
Cut 2 from white for "V."

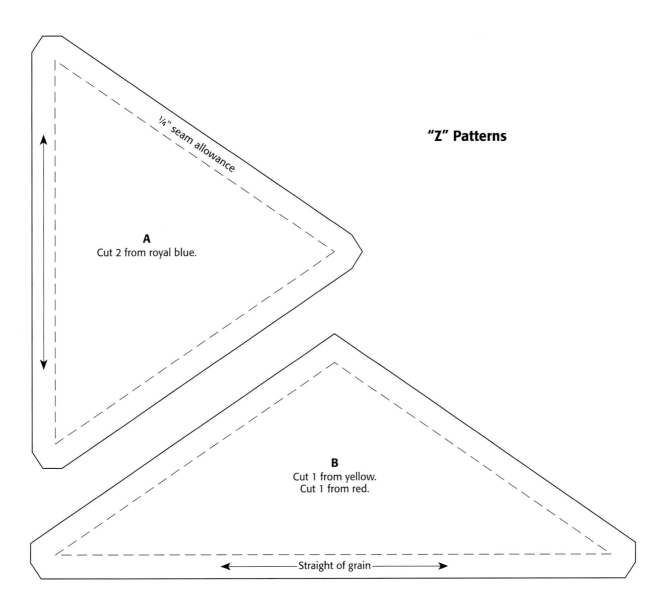

¼" seam allowance

"Z" Patterns

A
Cut 2 from royal blue.

B
Cut 1 from yellow.
Cut 1 from red.

Straight of grain

Big Red Checkerboard Star

By Mary Hickey. Quilted by Dawn Kelly.

Growing up in the country just west of St. Louis, Missouri, we always had a menagerie of animals. A shelf in the back of the shed held the boxes and bags of feed for all our farmyard friends. And every one of those bags and boxes had a red checkerboard on its side. How could one not learn to love the sight of a red checkerboard? Red and white checks were always associated with cheerful, clucking hens, frolicking puppies, and adorable, nuzzling kittens. So I set out to design a red checkerboard star symbolic of nurturing our little animals. I love the perky design of the Star block, with its eight star points and its four little extra corners. I discovered that the little corners were too hard to piece, so I folded red squares of fabric into triangles and tucked them into the seams to make them three-dimensional.

Finished quilt size: 55" x 68"
Finished block size: 10½" x 10½"

Materials

Yardages are based on 42"-wide fabrics.

- 1¾ yards of cream fabric for Checkerboard Star block backgrounds and sashing blocks
- 1¼ yards of cream-and-red fabric for sashing
- ⅞ yard of red fabric for inner and outer borders
- ⅞ yard of cream-and-red fabric for middle border
- ¾ yard *each* of four assorted red fabrics for blocks
- ⅜ yard of red fabric for sashing blocks
- ¼ yard *each* of four assorted cream-and-red fabrics for blocks
- ¼ yard of red fabric for prairie points
- 3⅝ yards of fabric for backing
- ⅞ yard of fabric for binding
- 58" x 71" piece of batting

Cutting

All measurements include ¼"-wide seam allowances.

From the cream fabric, cut:

2 strips, 12½" x 42"; crosscut into 4 squares, 12½" x 12½"

5 strips, 3½" x 42"; crosscut into 48 squares, 3½" x 3½"

3 strips, 2" x 42"; crosscut into 48 squares, 2" x 2"

2 strips, 3" x 42"; crosscut into 20 squares, 3" x 3"

From *each* of the four assorted red fabrics for blocks, cut:

2 strips, 2" x 42"

1 strip, 2" x 15"

1 square, 12½" x 12½"

From *each* of the four assorted cream-and-red fabrics for blocks, cut:

1 strip, 2" x 42"

2 strips, 2" x 15"

From the red fabric for prairie points, cut:

3 strips, 2" x 42"; crosscut into 48 squares,
  2½" x 2½"

From the red fabric for sashing blocks, cut:

4 strips, 1¾" x 42"; crosscut into 80 squares,
  1¾" x 1¾"

From the cream-and-red fabric for sashing, cut:

11 strips, 3" x 42"; crosscut into 31 rectangles,
  3" x 11"

**From the red fabric for inner and outer
borders, cut:**

12 strips, 2" x 42"

**From the cream-and-red fabric for the middle
border, cut:**

6 strips, 4" x 42"

From the binding fabric, cut:

256" of 2¼"-wide bias strips

Assembling the Checkerboard Star Blocks

1. Sew matching 2" x 15" assorted cream-and-red strips to both long sides of a 2" x 15" assorted red strip to make strip set A. Make four strip sets. Crosscut *each* strip set into six segments, 2" wide. Keep the segments from each strip set together.

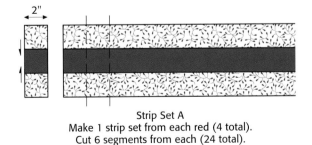

Strip Set A
Make 1 strip set from each red (4 total).
Cut 6 segments from each (24 total).

2. Using the same combination of fabrics that you used for the A strip sets, sew a 2" x 42" assorted red strip to both long sides of a 2" x 42"

cream-and-red print strip to make strip set B. Make four strip sets. Crosscut each strip set into 15 segments, 2" wide. Keep the segments from each strip set together.

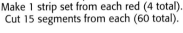
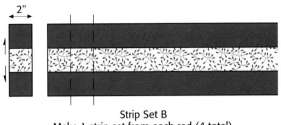

Strip Set B
Make 1 strip set from each red (4 total).
Cut 15 segments from each (60 total).

3. Using A and B segments from the same combination of fabrics, arrange two strip set A segments and one strip set B segment as shown. Sew the segments together to make a nine-patch unit. Make 12.

Make 12.

4. Refer to "Half-Square-Triangle Units" on page 5 to make half-square triangles. Pair each 12½" cream square with a 12½" red square. Cut the strips 2" wide. Cut 96 squares, 2" x 2".

5. To make the prairie points, fold the 2½" red squares in half diagonally, wrong sides together, and then in half diagonally again; press, using steam.

6. With the raw edges aligned, center a prairie point on the right side of each 2" cream square as shown.

7. Stitch matching half-square triangles to both sides of the prairie point units as shown. Trim the excess prairie point ends from the seam allowance. Make 12 sets of four matching units.

8. Stitch a matching strip set B segment to the bottom of each set of prairie point units as shown.

9. Arrange one nine-patch unit, four 3½" cream squares, and four prairie point units that match the nine-patch unit as shown to complete the Checkerboard Star block.

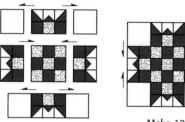

Make 12.

Assembling the Quilt Top

1. To make the sashing blocks, use a pencil and your rotary-cutting ruler to draw a diagonal line from corner to corner on the wrong side of each 1¾" red square. Place a marked square on opposite corners of a 3" cream square, right sides together, as shown. Stitch on the pencil lines. Trim ¼" from the stitching line. Flip open the triangles and press the seams toward the red triangles. Repeat on the opposite two corners of each square.

Make 20.

2. To make the sashing rows, stitch four sashing blocks and three 3" x 11" cream-and-red rectangles together as shown. Make five rows.

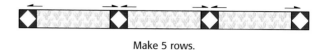

Make 5 rows.

3. To make the block rows, stitch four 3" x 11" cream-and-red rectangles and three blocks together as shown. Make four rows.

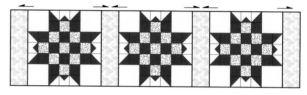

Make 4 rows.

4. Refer to the photo on page 66 to stitch the sashing and block rows together. Press the seams toward the sashing rows.

5. Refer to "Borders with Mitered Corners" on page 9 to make border units from the inner-, middle-, and outer-border strips. Press the seams toward the inner- and outer-border strips. Stitch the border units to the quilt top and miter the corners.

Finishing the Quilt

Refer to "Quiltmaking Techniques" on page 5 for details on quilt finishing, if needed.

1. Cut and piece the backing fabric so it is approximately 4" to 6" larger than the quilt top.

2. Layer the backing, batting, and quilt top; baste the layers together.

3. Hand or machine quilt as desired. The quilt shown was machine quilted with swoops, swirls, and swags.

4. Trim the batting and backing fabric even with the quilt top. Make a hanging sleeve and attach it to the quilt back.

5. Bind the quilt edges with the bias strips. Add a label to the quilt back.

Cleo's Cats

By Cleo Nollette. Quilted by Dawn Kelly.

The cats on our farm were plump, wide, portly, tubby, lumbering, burly, and well fed. Over the years of my childhood we had numerous cats, every one of which I loved with all my heart. My all-time favorites were a calico named Pansy and her best friend, a great tubby tabby named Hank. Pansy and Hank lived in the shed and guarded the red-checkerboard bags of animal feed from mice and other little varmints. Cleo, the gifted maker of this quilt, has two cats, Ginger and Poppy. They are not thin either. Like the cats in this quilt, they have wide, friendly faces and cool, demanding personalities. The Stepping Stone blocks are slightly unorthodox in that the four-patch units are a different size than the center square, but that just makes them easier to make, and of course, we are always in favor of anything easier.

Finished quilt size: 56½" x 72½"
Finished block size: 8" x 8"

Materials

Yardages are based on 42"-wide fabrics.

- 1½ yards of large-scale blue floral for outer border
- 1⅛ yards of natural tone-on-tone for Stepping Stone block backgrounds
- ½ yard of small-scale blue floral for Stepping Stone blocks
- ½ yard of rose print for inner border
- ⅜ yard of medium-scale blue floral for Stepping Stone blocks
- Scraps no smaller than 10" x 10" of 18 assorted white fabrics for Cat block backgrounds
- Scraps no smaller than 8" x 10" of 18 assorted dark prints for Cat blocks
- 3¾ yards of fabric for backing
- ⅞ yard of fabric for binding
- 60" x 76" piece of batting
- 3 pairs of ⅜"-diameter buttons for cats' eyes

Cutting

All measurements include ¼"-wide seam allowances.

From the natural tone-on-tone, cut:
7 strips, 1¾" x 42"
4 strips, 3½" x 42"
3 strips, 3" x 42"

From the small-scale blue floral, cut:
7 strips, 1¾" x 42"

From the medium-scale blue floral, cut:
2 strips, 3½" x 42"

From *each* of the 18 assorted white fabrics, cut:
2 rectangles, 2¾" x 5"
1 rectangle, 1½" x 4"
2 rectangles, 1¾" x 4"
4 squares, 1¼" x 1¼"
2 squares, 1½" x 1½"

From *each* of the 18 assorted dark fabrics, cut:
1 rectangle, 4" x 5½"
1 rectangle, 2½" x 4"
2 squares, 1¼" x 1¼"
2 rectangles, 1½" x 4"

69

From the rose print, cut:

6 strips, 1¾" x 42"

From the *lengthwise* grain of the large-scale blue floral, cut:

2 strips, 7¼" x 63"

2 strips, 7¼" x 60"

From the binding fabric, cut:

268" of 2¼"-wide bias strips

Assembling the Stepping Stone Blocks

1. Sew a 1¾" x 42" natural strip to one long side of each 1¾" x 42" small-scale blue floral strip to make a strip set. Make seven strip sets. Crosscut the strip sets into 136 segments, 1¾" wide.

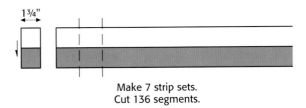

Make 7 strip sets.
Cut 136 segments.

2. Stitch two segments together as shown to make a four-patch unit. Make 68.

Make 68.

3. Sew a 3½" x 42" natural strip to both long sides of a 3½" x 42" medium-scale blue floral strip to make a strip set. Make two. Crosscut the strip sets into 17 segments, 3½" wide.

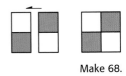

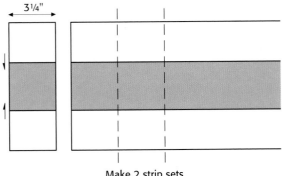

Make 2 strip sets.
Cut 17 segments.

4. With right sides together, arrange four-patch units on the top edge of a 3" x 42" natural strip, being careful to orient the blue squares in the four-patch units as shown. Allow a small amount of space between each four-patch unit. Stitch along the long edge. Press the seam toward the natural strip. Place your ruler on the strip so it spans the natural strip and the four-patch unit. Align your rotary-cutting ruler with the right edge of the four-patch unit and cut across the strip. Trim the left side of each segment even with the four-patch unit.

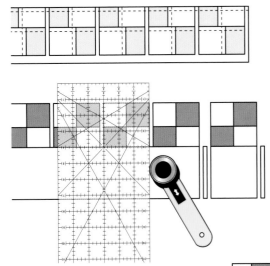

5. Stitch a four-patch unit to the bottom of each unit from step 4, being careful to orient the four patch as shown.

6. Stitch one segment from step 3 and two four-patch units from step 4 together as shown to complete the Stepping Stone blocks.

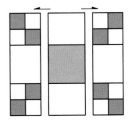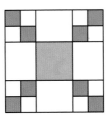

Make 17.

Assembling the Cat Blocks

Note: Each block is made using the pieces from one of the assorted white fabrics for the background and the pieces from one of the assorted dark fabrics for the cat.

1. To make each block, use a pencil to draw a diagonal line from corner to corner on the wrong side of the four 1¼" white squares. Place two of the marked squares on the bottom right and left corners of the 2½" x 4" dark rectangle as shown, right sides together. Stitch on the marked lines. Trim ¼" from the stitching line. Flip open the triangles and press the seams toward the dark.

Cheeks

2. Place the remaining marked squares on the upper corners of the 4" x 5½" dark rectangle as shown, right sides together. Stitch, trim, and press as before.

Body

3. Draw a diagonal line from corner to corner on the wrong side of the two 1¼" dark squares. Place the marked squares on opposite corners of the 1½" x 4" white rectangle as shown, right sides together. Stitch, trim, and press as before.

Ears

4. Draw a diagonal line from corner to corner on the wrong side of the two 1½" white squares. Place the marked squares on opposite corners of the two 1½" x 4" dark rectangles as shown, right sides together. Stitch, trim, and press as before.

Hips

5. Arrange the units from steps 1–4, the two 2¾" x 5" white rectangles, and the two 1¾" x 4" white rectangles as shown. Stitch the pieces together in vertical rows and then stitch the rows together to complete the Cat block. Press the seams toward the cat's body.

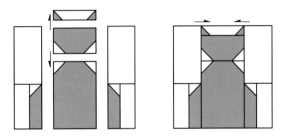

6. Repeat steps 1–5 to make a total of 18 Cat blocks.

Assembling the Quilt Top

1. Refer to the quilt assembly diagram on page 74 to arrange the blocks in seven rows of five blocks each, alternating the Cat blocks and Stepping Stone blocks in each row and from row to row.

2. Stitch the blocks in each row together; press the seams toward the Cat blocks. Stitch the rows together; press the seams in one direction.

3. Refer to "Appliqué Methods" on page 6 to make three tails from the remainder of the dark fabrics, using the pattern on page 74 and the desired appliqué method. Appliqué the tails to the base of the corresponding-color Cat block, referring to the photo on page 72 for placement as needed.

4. Refer to "Borders with Straight-Sewn Corners" on page 8 to join and trim the rose-print strips to the correct lengths and stitch them to the quilt top. Press the seams toward the border strips. Measure the quilt for the outer side borders. Trim the 7¼" x 63" large-scale blue floral strips to the correct length and stitch them to the quilt top. Measure the quilt top for the outer top and bottom borders. Trim the 7¼" x 60" blue floral strips to the correct length and stitch them to the quilt top and bottom edges. Press the seams toward the rose border strips.

Quilt Assembly

Finishing the Quilt

Refer to "Quiltmaking Techniques" on page 5 for details on quilt finishing, if needed.

1. Cut and piece the backing fabric so it is approximately 4" to 6" larger than the quilt top.

2. Layer the backing, batting, and quilt top; baste the layers together.

3. Hand or machine quilt as desired. The quilt shown was machine quilted with swoops, swirls, and swags.

4. Stitch the buttons to three of the Cat blocks for eyes.

5. Trim the batting and backing fabric even with the quilt top. Make a hanging sleeve and attach it to the quilt back.

6. Bind the quilt edges with the bias strips. Add a label to the quilt back.

Appliqué Pattern

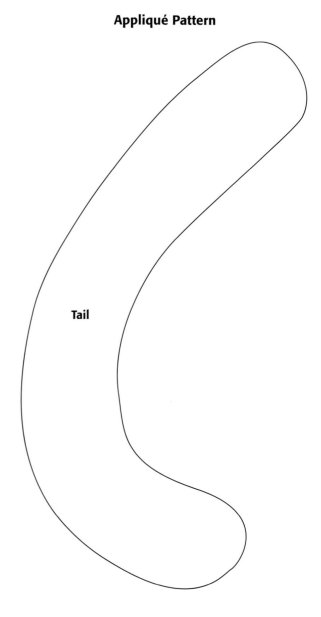

Tail

Little Egg Baskets

By Mary Hickey. Quilted by Fannie Schwartz.

I'm not sure if I called this "Little Egg Baskets" because the baskets could hold eggs collected from under hens or if it's because the baskets are shaped like eggs. Either way, the baskets and their sweet little bouquets are adorable. The colors in the backgrounds of this quilt are very delicate and the contrast slight. Somehow, the pale mint greens and soft sky blues are very pleasing to the eye. The outer border, while made up of Nine Patch blocks, is really visually made of the darker blue squares in the nine patches. The rest of the colors and patches just add width, interest, space, and beauty.

Finished quilt size: 42½" x 42½"
Finished appliqué block size: 11½" x 11½"
Finished border block size: 4½" x 4½"

Materials

Yardages are based on 42"-wide fabrics.

- 1 yard of pale green fabric for Appliqué block backgrounds and border blocks
- ½ yard of pale blue fabric for Appliqué block backgrounds and border blocks
- ½ yard of medium green fabric for border setting triangles
- ½ yard of white fabric for border setting triangles
- ½ yard of light tan fabric for baskets
- ⅜ yard of medium blue fabric for border blocks and outer border
- ⅜ yard of dark blue fabric for border blocks
- ⅜ yard of dark green plaid for stems
- Scraps of dark pink, light pink, dark blue, light blue, dark yellow, and assorted green fabrics for appliqué flowers and leaves
- 2⅞ yards of fabric for backing
- ⅞ yard of fabric for binding
- 46" x 46" piece of batting

- ⅜"- and ½"-wide bias bars
- 1¼ yards of paper-backed fusible web for fusible-web appliqué **OR** lightweight cotton or interfacing for face-and-turn appliqué

Cutting

All measurements include ¼"-wide seam allowances.

From the pale blue fabric, cut:
5 strips, 1¾" x 42"; crosscut into:
  8 strips, 1¾" x 9½"
  8 strips, 1¾" x 12"
2 strips, 2" x 42"

From the pale green fabric, cut:
1 strip, 9½" x 42"; crosscut into 4 squares, 9½" x 9½"
2 strips, 2½" x 42"; crosscut into:
  2 strips, 2½" x 12"
  1 strip, 2½" x 25½"
5 strips, 2" x 42"
3 strips, 1½" x 42"; crosscut into:
  2 strips, 1½" x 25½"
  2 strips, 1½" x 27½"

From the dark green plaid, cut:

18" of 1⅜"-wide bias strips

50" of 1⅛"-wide bias strips

From the dark blue fabric, cut:

4 strips, 2" x 42"

From the medium blue fabric, cut:

1 strip, 2" x 42"

5 strips, 1½" x 42"

From the medium green fabric, cut:

4 squares, 7¾" x 7¾"; cut each square in half twice diagonally to yield 16 triangles

6 squares, 4¼" x 4¼"; cut each square in half once diagonally to yield 12 triangles

From the white fabric, cut:

4 squares, 7¾" x 7¾"; cut each square in half twice diagonally to yield 16 triangles

2 squares, 4¼" x 4¼"; cut each square in half once diagonally to yield 4 triangles

From the binding fabric, cut:

182" of 2¼"-wide bias strips

Assembling the Quilt-Top Center

1. Stitch the 1¾" x 9½" pale blue strips to the sides of each pale green 9½" square. Stitch the 1¾" x 12" pale blue strips to the top and bottom of each square.

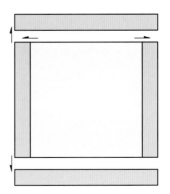

2. Arrange the squares from step 1 into two vertical rows of two blocks each. Stitch a 2½" x 12" pale green strip between the blocks in each row as shown. Stitch the rows together, adding the 2½" x 25½" pale green strip between them.

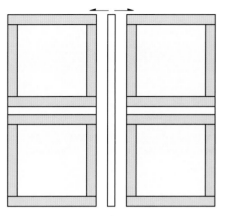

3. Stitch the 1½" x 25½" pale green strips to the sides of the block unit from step 2. Stitch the 1½" x 27½" pale green strips to the top and bottom of the unit.

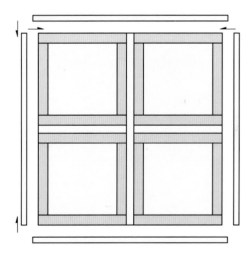

4. Stitch the 1⅜"-wide plaid strips together end to end to make one long strip. Follow the manufacturer's instructions to use the ½"-wide bias bar to make a bias tube. Cut the tube into four 3½" lengths for the posies' stems. In the same manner, stitch the 1⅛"-wide plaid strips together and use the ⅜"-wide bias bar to make a tube. Cut the tube

into four 2" lengths for the dark blue tulips' stems, four 2½" lengths for the light blue tulips' stems, and four 3½" lengths for the lilies' stems.

5. Refer to "Appliqué Methods" on page 6 to make the basket, flower, and leaf appliqué shapes using patterns A–H on pages 79 and 80 and the desired appliqué method. Apply them and the stems from step 4 to the quilt top center. Refer to the quilt assembly diagram and the photo on page 76 for placement as needed.

Assembling the Borders

1. Stitch a 2" x 42" pale green strip to both long edges of a 2" x 42" dark blue strip as shown to make one strip set A. Crosscut the strip set into 20 segments, 2" wide.

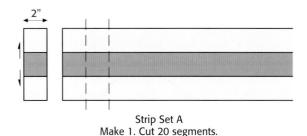

Strip Set A
Make 1. Cut 20 segments.

2. Stitch 2" x 42" dark blue, pale green, and pale blue strips together as shown to make strip set B. Make two. Crosscut the strip sets into 24 segments, 2" wide.

Strip Set B
Make 2. Cut 24 segments.

3. Stitch 2" x 42" medium blue, pale green, and dark blue strips together as shown to make one strip set C. Crosscut the strip set into 16 segments, 2" wide.

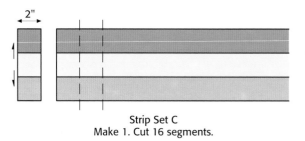

Strip Set C
Make 1. Cut 16 segments.

4. Assemble the segments as shown to make the two different Nine Patch blocks. Make the number of blocks indicated for each combination.

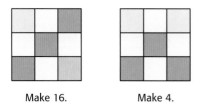

Make 16.   Make 4.

5. Arrange the border blocks and medium green and white print triangles as shown to make the side and top/bottom border units. Stitch the pieces together in diagonal rows and then stitch the rows together. Make two of each.

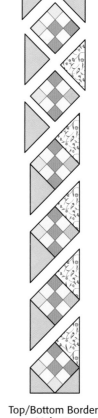

Side Border
Make 2.

Top/Bottom Border
Make 2.

Assembling the Quilt Top

1. Refer to the quilt assembly diagram to stitch the side borders to the sides of the quilt-top center. Stitch the top and bottom borders to the top and bottom edges of the quilt-top center.

2. Refer to "Borders with Straight-Sewn Corners" on page 8 to join and trim the medium blue 1½" x 42" strips to the correct lengths and stitch them to the quilt top. Press the seams toward the border strips.

Finishing the Quilt

Refer to "Quiltmaking Techniques" on page 5 for details on quilt finishing, if needed.

1. Cut and piece the backing fabric so it is approximately 4" to 6" larger than the quilt top.

2. Layer the backing, batting, and quilt top; baste the layers together.

3. Hand or machine quilt as desired. The quilt shown was hand quilted with in-the-ditch quilting, diagonal lines, and a little scroll design.

4. Trim the batting and backing fabric even with the quilt top. Make a hanging sleeve and attach it to the quilt back.

5. Bind the quilt edges with the bias strips. Add a label to the quilt back.

Quilt Assembly

Appliqué Patterns

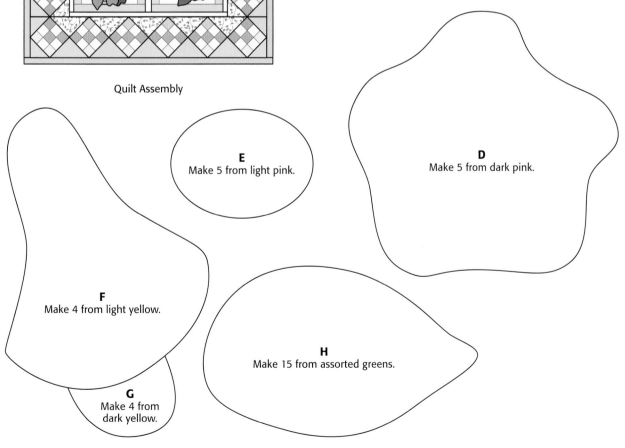

E
Make 5 from light pink.

D
Make 5 from dark pink.

F
Make 4 from light yellow.

H
Make 15 from assorted greens.

G
Make 4 from dark yellow.

Appliqué Patterns and
Placement Guide

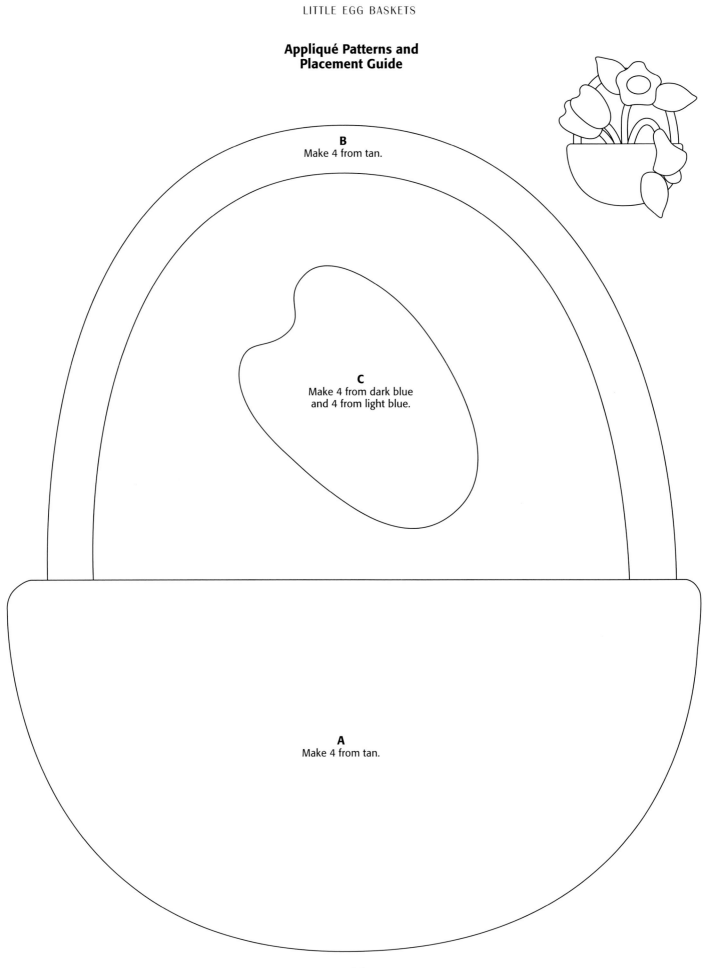

B
Make 4 from tan.

C
Make 4 from dark blue
and 4 from light blue.

A
Make 4 from tan.

Cherry Orchard Farms

By Mary Hickey. Quilted by Judy Irish.

The center of this block is really just a traditional Snowball block with a cluster of cherries, a bunch of strawberries, or a cheerful songbird machine appliquéd to the middle of the block. After making the snowball part of the block, add a pieced frame that includes eight quick corners in dark green, and the block takes on a strong circular look. So while the quilt looks fairly complex, the piecing is really very easy—just straight seams and quick corners. The scalloped border is great fun to make and elevates the blocks to a little masterpiece of cottage style.

Finished quilt size: 57½" x 57½"
Finished block size: 11½" x 11½"

Materials

Yardages are based on 42"-wide fabrics.

- 2⅜ yards of off-white fabric for block backgrounds, sashing pieces, and scalloped border
- 1⅜ yards of red fabric for outer border
- ¾ yard of light green fabric for blocks
- ⅝ yard of dark green fabric for blocks
- ⅝ yard of light pink fabric for sashing
- ⅜ yard of dark pink fabric for sashing squares and inner border
- ⅜ yard of medium pink fabric for block corners
- Scraps of light, medium, and dark red fabrics for strawberry and cherry appliqués
- Scraps of light, medium, and dark green fabrics for leaf appliqués
- Scrap of blue fabric for bird appliqués
- 3¾ yards of fabric for backing
- ⅞ yard of fabric for binding
- 61" x 61" piece of batting
- Posterboard
- Freezer paper
- ½ yard of paper-backed fusible web

Cutting

All measurements include ¼"-wide seam allowances.

From the dark green fabric, cut:
3 strips, 2¾" x 42"; crosscut into 36 squares, 2¾" x 2¾"
4 strips, 2" x 42"; crosscut into 72 squares, 2" x 2"

From the off-white fabric, cut:
3 strips, 8" x 42"; crosscut into 9 squares, 8" x 8"
4 strips, 2½" x 42"
10 strips, 4" x 42"

From the light green fabric, cut:
8 strips, 2½" x 42"; crosscut into 72 rectangles, 2½" x 4¼"

From the medium pink fabric, cut:
3 strips, 2½" x 42"; crosscut into 36 squares, 2½" x 2½"

From the light pink fabric, cut:
2 strips, 8" x 42"

From the dark pink fabric, cut:
1 strip, 2½" x 42"; crosscut into 16 squares, 2½" x 2½"
5 strips, 1¼" x 42"

From the red fabric, cut:
6 strips, 7" x 42"

From the binding fabric, cut:
240" of 2¼"-wide bias strips

Assembling the Blocks

1. Using a pencil and your rotary-cutting ruler, draw a diagonal line from corner to corner on the wrong side of each 2¾" dark green square. Place the marked squares on each corner of each 8" off-white square as shown, right sides together. Stitch on the marked lines. Trim ¼" from the stitching line. Flip open the triangles and press the seams toward the dark green.

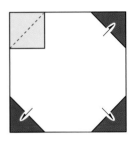

2. Refer to "Fusible-Web Appliqué" on page 7 to make appliqué shapes A–G on pages 87 and 88 and apply them to the 8" off-white squares. Refer to the quilt assembly diagram and the photo on page 84 for placement as needed. Using a slightly darker shade of thread than the appliqué shape, blanket stitch around the shapes by hand or machine.

3. Draw a diagonal line from corner to corner on the wrong side of each dark green 2" square. Place a marked square on the upper-right corner of 36 light green 2½" x 4¼" rectangles as shown, right sides together. Take care to orient the marked squares as shown. Stitch on the marked lines. Trim ¼" from the stitching line. Flip open the triangles and press the seams toward the dark green. Repeat to make 36 rectangles with the dark green triangle on the upper-left corner.

Make 36.   Make 36.

4. Stitch the rectangles into pairs as shown so the dark green triangles meet.

5. Sew a rectangle unit from step 4 to the top and bottom edges of each appliquéd square so that the triangles are pointing out. Sew a 2½" medium pink square to each end of the remaining rectangle units. Stitch these units to the sides of the appliquéd squares as shown to complete the blocks.

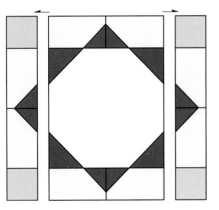

83

Assembling the Quilt Top

1. Stitch a 2½" x 42" off-white strip to both long sides of an 8" x 42" light pink strip to make a strip set. Make two. Crosscut the strip sets into 24 segments, 2½" wide.

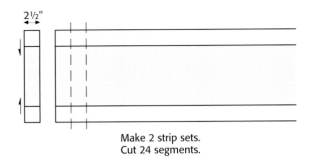

Make 2 strip sets.
Cut 24 segments.

2. To make the block rows, refer to the quilt assembly diagram to arrange the blocks into three horizontal rows of three blocks each. Stitch a segment from step 1 between each block and at the beginning and end of each row as shown. Press the seams toward the blocks.

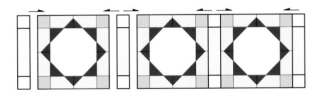

3. To make the sashing rows, stitch three segments from step 1 and four 2½" dark pink squares together as shown. Press the seams toward the dark pink squares. Make four rows.

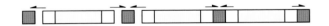

4. Refer to the quilt assembly diagram to stitch the sashing and block rows together as shown. Press the seams toward the sashing rows.

5. Refer to "Borders with Straight-Sewn Corners" on page 8 to join and trim the 1¼" x 42" dark pink strips to the correct lengths and stitch them to the quilt top. Press the seams toward the border strips.

6. Join the 4" x 42" off-white strips end to end. From the joined strip, cut eight strips, 4" x 49½".

7. Trace the scallop pattern on page 87 onto posterboard. Cut four strips of freezer paper 5" x 50". Layer the four pieces of freezer paper one on top of the other, dull side up; pin together in several places. Using a pencil and the scallop template, trace 13 full scallops onto the top piece of paper. Use paper scissors to cut out the scalloped strips. Place a freezer paper strip, shiny side down, on the wrong side of four of the strips from step 6. Align the straight edge of the paper with the straight edge of the fabric strips; use an iron to press the paper in place. Pin each strip, right sides together, with the remaining off-white strips from step 6.

8. Using a very small stitch length, sew around the scallops of the paper pattern. When you reach the valley at the base of each scallop, leave the needle in the down position, pivot the fabric to the side, take two stitches, leave the needle in the down position, pivot the fabric to start the next scallop, and then continue to sew the rest of the scallop. Remove the paper pattern.

9. Using pinking shears, trim the scallops close to the stitching. With sharp scissors, clip close to but not through the stitches in the valleys. Turn the scallops right side out. Make a cardboard template the shape of the scallops, slide it into each scallop, and while it is in place, press the scallop.

10. Press a crease in the center of each scallop strip and the center of each side of the quilt top. Refer to "Borders with Mitered Corners" on page 9 to align the center marks and baste the scalloped strips to the quilt top.

    Note: I mitered the corners of the scallops at this time. You can stitch the miters now or wait and miter the corners at the same time as the outer border.

11. Refer to "Borders with Mitered Corners" to join and trim the 7" x 42" red strips to the correct lengths. These borders are attached to the quilt top in the same seam as the scalloped border. Adjust the borders so that the corners match nicely when mitered. Stitch the borders to the quilt top and miter the corners.

Finishing the Quilt

Refer to "Quiltmaking Techniques" on page 5 for details on quilt finishing, if needed.

1. Cut and piece the backing fabric so it is approximately 4" to 6" larger than the quilt top.

2. Layer the backing, batting, and quilt top; baste the layers together.

3. Hand or machine quilt as desired. The quilt shown was machine quilted with vines, flowers, loops, and birds.

4. Trim the batting and backing fabric even with the quilt top. Make a hanging sleeve and attach it to the quilt back.

5. Bind the quilt edges with the bias strips. Add a label to the quilt back.

Quilt Assembly

Appliqué Patterns

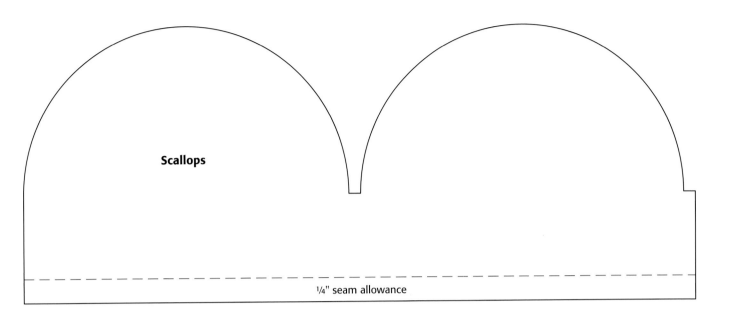

Scallops

¼" seam allowance

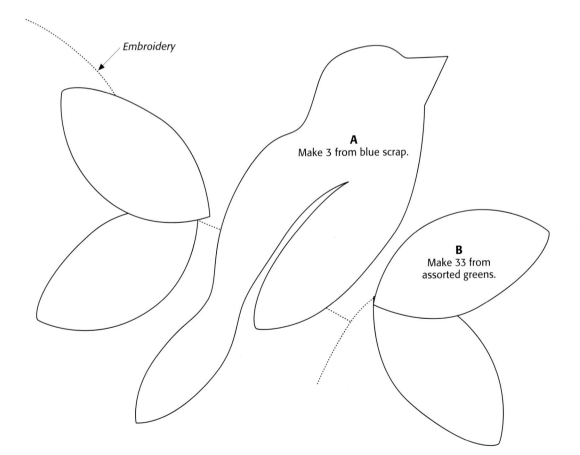

Embroidery

A
Make 3 from blue scrap.

B
Make 33 from
assorted greens.

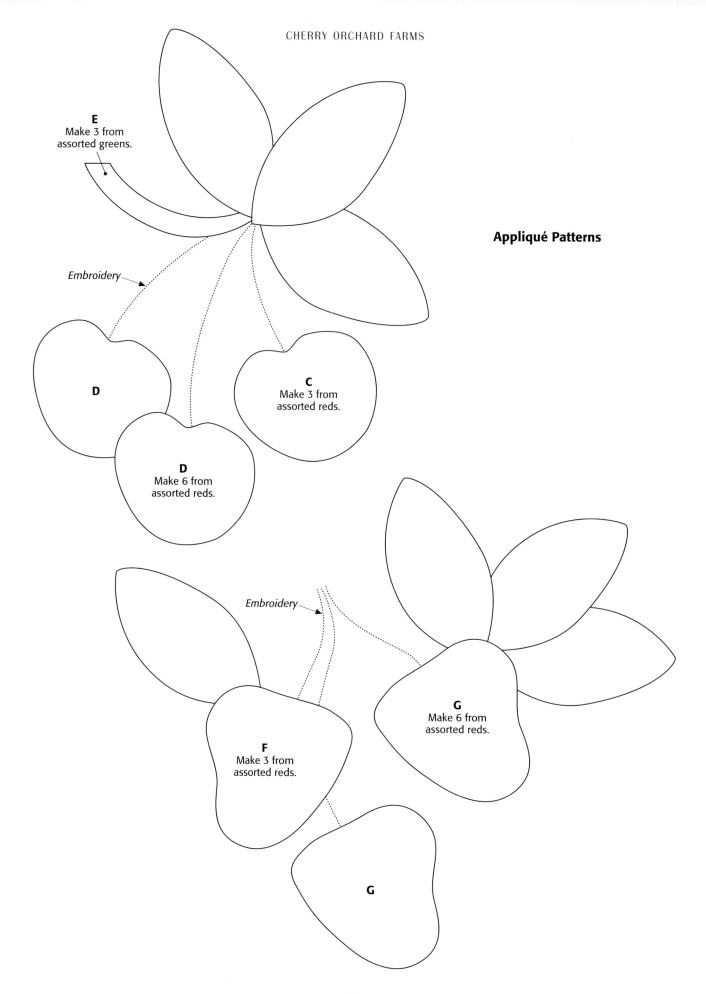

E
Make 3 from
assorted greens.

Appliqué Patterns

Embroidery

D

C
Make 3 from
assorted reds.

D
Make 6 from
assorted reds.

Embroidery

G
Make 6 from
assorted reds.

F
Make 3 from
assorted reds.

G

Mountain Double Nine Patch

By Mary Hickey. Quilted by Dawn Kelly.

The simplicity of the Double Nine Patch block is much beloved by quilters. It's direct, straightforward, and always makes a striking quilt. This quilt has dark red Double Nine Patch blocks alternating with simple coral and peach triangle blocks, creating an interesting and yet very easy quilt. I arranged the colors of the triangle blocks to make a diagonal square embracing the dark red Double Nine Patch blocks. This technique takes what could be an ordinary quilt to a stunning level, adding interest and depth to the quilt without creating additional difficulty.

Finished quilt size: 81" x 81"
Finished block size: 9" x 9"

Materials

Yardages are based on 42"-wide fabrics.

- 2⅝ yards of rust floral for outer border
- ⅜ yard *each* of 5 assorted dark red fabrics for Double Nine Patch blocks
- 1⅜ yards of peach fabric for Half-Square Triangle and Alternate Triangle blocks
- 1⅛ yards *total* of assorted off-white fabrics for Double Nine Patch blocks
- 1 yard of unbleached muslin for Double Nine Patch blocks
- 1 yard of coral fabrics for Half-Square Triangle and Alternate Triangle blocks
- ½ yard of pale pink fabric for Alternate Triangle blocks
- 7¼ yards of fabric for backing
- 1 yard of fabric for binding
- 85" x 85" piece of batting

Cutting

All measurements include ¼"-wide seam allowances.

From each of the 5 assorted dark red fabrics, cut:
5 strips, 1½" x 42"

From the muslin, cut:
20 strips, 1½" x 42"

From the assorted off-white fabrics, cut a *total* of:
9 strips, 3½" x 42"; crosscut 3 into 25 squares, 3½" x 3½"

From the coral fabric, cut:
2 strips, 10" x 42"; crosscut into 8 squares, 10" x 10"
1 strip, 10¼" x 42"; crosscut into 3 squares, 10¼" x 10¼"

From the peach fabric, cut:
2 strips, 10" x 42"; crosscut into 8 squares, 10" x 10"
2 strips, 10¼" x 42"; crosscut into 4 squares, 10¼" x 10¼"

From the pale pink fabric, cut:
1 square, 10¼" x 10¼"

From the *lengthwise* grain of the rust floral, cut:
2 strips, 9¼" x 68"
2 strips, 9¼" x 85"

From the binding fabric, cut:
336" of 2¼"-wide bias strips

Assembling the Double Nine Patch Blocks

1. Sew matching 1½" x 42" dark red strips to both long sides of a 1½" x 42" muslin strip to make strip set A. Make two strip sets from each red (10 total). Crosscut each pair of strip sets into 50 segments (250 total), 1½" wide.

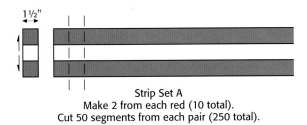

Strip Set A
Make 2 from each red (10 total).
Cut 50 segments from each pair (250 total).

2. Sew a 1½" x 42" muslin strip to both long sides of the remaining red strips to make strip set B. Make one strip set from each red (five total). Crosscut each strip set into 25 segments (125 total), 1½" wide.

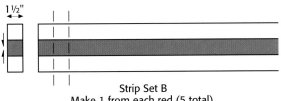

Strip Set B
Make 1 from each red (5 total).
Cut 25 segments from each (125 total).

3. Using segments with the same red, arrange two strip set A segments and one strip set B segment as shown. Sew the segments together to make a small nine-patch unit. Make 25 from each red print (125 total).

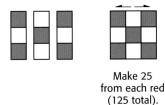

Make 25
from each red
(125 total).

4. With right sides together, place 75 of the small nine-patch units side by side along one long edge of six of the 3½" x 42" off-white strips as shown, leaving a small amount of space between each unit. Stitch along the long edge. Press the seams toward the off-white strips. Align your rotary-cutting ruler with the right edge of each small nine-patch unit and cut across the off-white strip. Trim the left edge of the strip even with the left edge of the nine-patch unit.

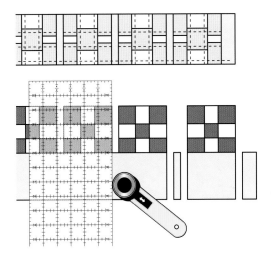

5. Stitch one of the remaining small nine-patch units from step 3 to 50 of the units from step 4 as shown.

Make 50.

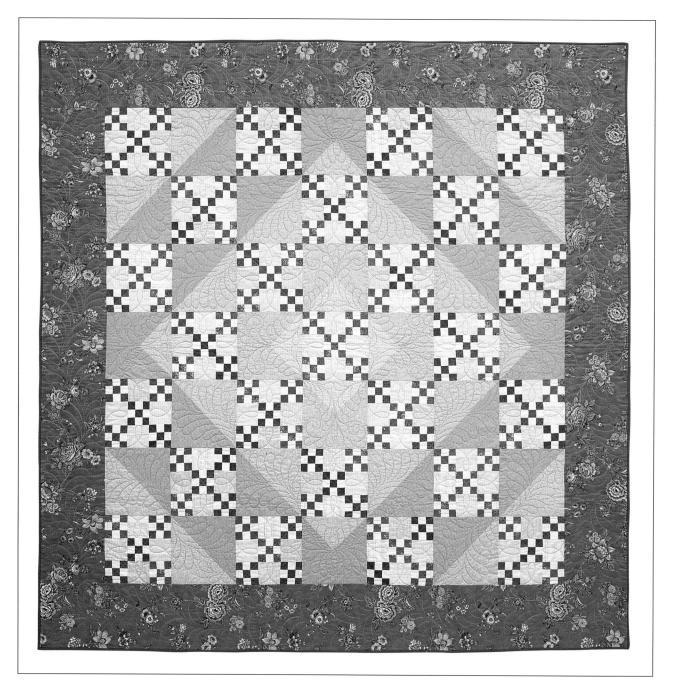

6. Stitch a 3½" off-white square to each of the remaining 25 units from step 4 as shown.

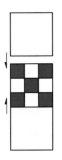

Make 25.

7. Stitch two units from step 5 and one unit from step 6 together as shown to complete the Double Nine Patch blocks. Make 25.

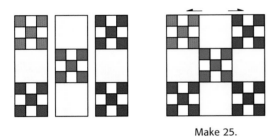

Make 25.

Assembling the Half-Square-Triangle and Alternate Triangle Blocks

1. To make the Half-Square-Triangle blocks, place each coral 10" square right sides together with a peach 10" square. Using a pencil and your rotary-cutting ruler, draw a diagonal line from corner to corner on the wrong side of the peach squares. Stitch ¼" from both sides of the line. Cut the squares apart on the marked line, flip open the squares, and press the seams toward the coral. Make 16. Trim the blocks to 9½" x 9½".

Make 16.

2. To make the Alternate Triangle blocks, cut two peach and two coral 10¼" squares in half diagonally to make four triangles of each color. Set the triangles aside.

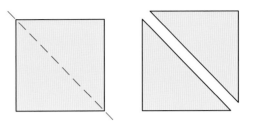

3. Repeat step 1 with one pale pink and one peach 10¼" square to make two half-square triangles; stitch the triangles together and press the seams toward the peach. Repeat with one peach and one coral 10¼" square to make two half-square triangles; press the seams toward the coral.

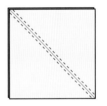

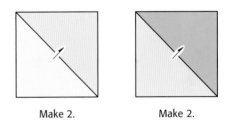

Make 2.　　　　Make 2.

4. Cut the half-square triangles from step 3 in half diagonally as shown.

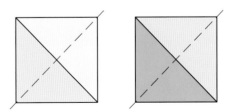

5. Sew the triangles from step 2 to the units from step 4 as shown. Trim the squares to 9½" x 9½".

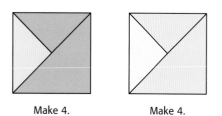

Make 4.   Make 4.

Assembling the Quilt Top

1. Refer to the quilt assembly diagram to arrange the blocks into seven horizontal rows of seven blocks each as shown.

2. Stitch the blocks in each row together; press the seams toward the Half-Square-Triangle and Alternate Triangle blocks. Sew the rows together; press the seams in one direction.

3. Refer to "Borders with Straight-Sewn Corners" on page 8 to trim the rust floral 9¼" x 68" strips to the correct lengths and stitch them to the sides of the quilt top. Trim

the 9¼" x 85" strips to the correct length and stitch them to the top and bottom edges of the quilt top. Press the seams toward the border strips.

Finishing the Quilt

Refer to "Quiltmaking Techniques" on page 5 for details on quilt finishing, if needed.

1. Cut and piece the backing fabric so it is approximately 4" to 6" larger than the quilt top.

2. Layer the backing, batting, and quilt top; baste the layers together.

3. Hand or machine quilt as desired. The quilt shown was machine quilted with feathered scrolls in the Triangle blocks, loops in the Double Nine Patch blocks, and a wavy feather motif in the border.

4. Trim the batting and backing even with the quilt top. Make a hanging sleeve and attach it to the quilt back.

5. Bind the quilt edges with the bias strips. Add a label to the quilt back.

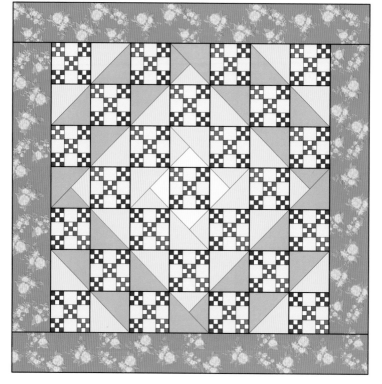

Quilt Assembly

Ancient Friendships

By Mary Hickey. Quilted by Dawn Kelly.

Symbolizing the bonds of friendship, the spiral linked to a hand is a pictogram from ancient Mexican and Southwest Indian art and folklore. In this quilt, the symbols are intertwined in the large spaces of the Delectable Mountains blocks. The quilt is predominantly tans and browns, with teal acting as the perfect complement to the color scheme. Curl up in this quilt by a cozy fire and picture yourself in a cabin high in the desert mountains.

Finished quilt size: 71½" x 85¾"
Finished block size: 10" x 10"

Materials

Yardages are based on 42"-wide fabrics.

- 2⅞ yards *total* of assorted beige prints for large and small half-square triangles
- 2⅜ yards *total* of assorted brown prints for small half-square triangles and setting triangles
- 1½ yards of brown print for outer border
- 1⅛ yards of assorted tan batiks for large half-square triangles
- 1 yard *total* of assorted teal prints for small half-square triangles and appliqués
- ⅝ yard of teal prints for inner border
- 5¼ yards of fabric for backing
- 1 yard of fabric for binding
- 75" x 90" piece of batting
- ¾ yard of paper-backed fusible web for fusible-web appliqué **OR** lightweight cotton or interfacing for face-and-turn appliqué

Cutting

All measurements include ¼"-wide seam allowances.

From the assorted brown prints, cut a *total* of:
7 squares, 12½" x 12½"

4 squares, 15½" x 15½"; cut each square in half twice diagonally to yield 16 side setting triangles. You will use 14 and have 2 left over.

2 squares, 8" x 8"; cut each square in half once diagonally to yield 4 corner setting triangles

From the assorted teal prints, cut a *total* of:
3 squares, 12½" x 12½"

From the assorted beige prints, cut:
4 strips, 9" x 42"; crosscut into 16 squares, 9" x 9"

4 strips, 12½" x 42"; crosscut into 10 squares, 12½" x 12½"

2 strips, 2½" x 42"; crosscut into 32 squares, 2½" x 2½"

From the assorted tan batiks, cut a *total* of:
16 squares, 9" x 9"

From the inner-border teal print, cut:
7 strips, 2¼" x 42"

From the outer-border brown print, cut:
8 strips, 5¾" x 42"

From the binding fabric, cut:
325" of 2¼"-wide bias strips

Assembling the Delectable Mountains Blocks

1. Refer to "Half-Square-Triangle Units" on page 5 to make the small half-square triangles. Pair each 12½" assorted brown and teal square with a 12½" assorted beige square. Cut the strips 2½" wide. Cut 77 teal/beige half-square triangles and 179 brown/beige half-square triangles.

2. Place each 9" tan batik square right sides together with a 9" beige square. Using a pencil and your rotary-cutting ruler, draw a diagonal line from corner to corner on the wrong side of each beige square. Stitch ¼" from both sides of the marked line. Cut the squares apart on the marked line, flip open the squares, and press the seams toward the tan. Make 32 large half-square triangles. Trim the squares to 8½" x 8½".

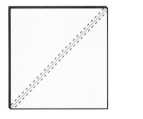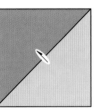

Make 32.

3. Arrange one large half-square triangle, eight assorted small half-square triangles, and one 2½" beige square as shown to complete the Delectable Mountains blocks. Make 32.

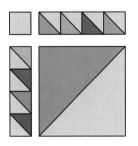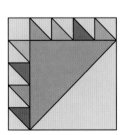

Make 32.

Assembling the Quilt Top

1. Refer to the quilt assembly diagram to arrange the blocks and side setting triangles into diagonal rows as shown.

2. Stitch the pieces in each row together; press the seams toward the blocks. Stitch the rows together; press the seams in one direction. Add the corner triangles to each corner.

3. Refer to "Appliqué Methods" on page 6 to make the appliqué shapes and apply them to the quilt top using patterns A–F on pages 99–101 and the desired method. Refer to the quilt assembly diagram and the photo on page 98 for placement as needed.

4. Refer to "Borders with Straight-Sewn Corners" on page 8 to join and trim the teal inner-border strips to the correct lengths and stitch them to the quilt top. Press the seams toward the border strips. Repeat with the brown outer-border strips. Press the seams toward the inner-border strips.

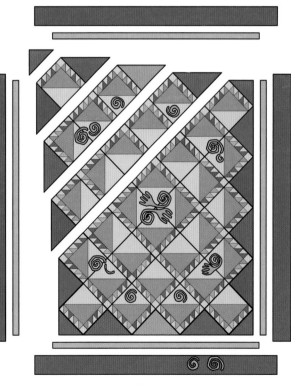

Quilt Assembly

Finishing the Quilt

Refer to "Quiltmaking Techniques" on page 5 for details on quilt finishing, if needed.

1. Cut and piece the backing fabric so it is approximately 4" to 6" larger than the quilt top.

2. Layer the backing, batting, and quilt top; baste the layers together.

3. Hand or machine quilt as desired. The quilt shown was machine quilted with spirals, arcs, and flames.

4. Trim the batting and backing even with the quilt top. Make a hanging sleeve and attach it to the quilt back.

5. Bind the quilt edges with the bias strips. Add a label to the quilt back.

Appliqué Pattern

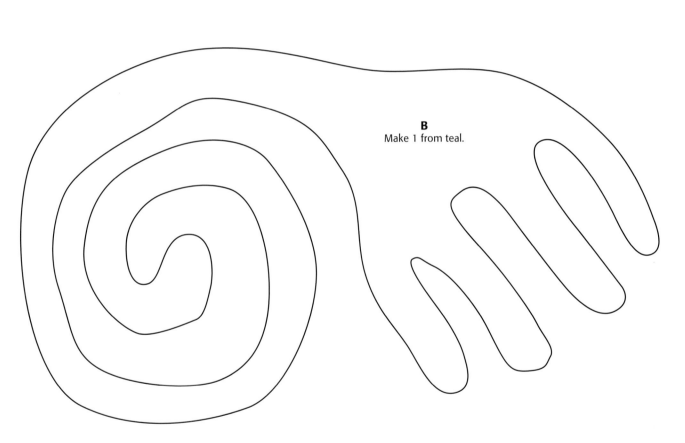

B
Make 1 from teal.

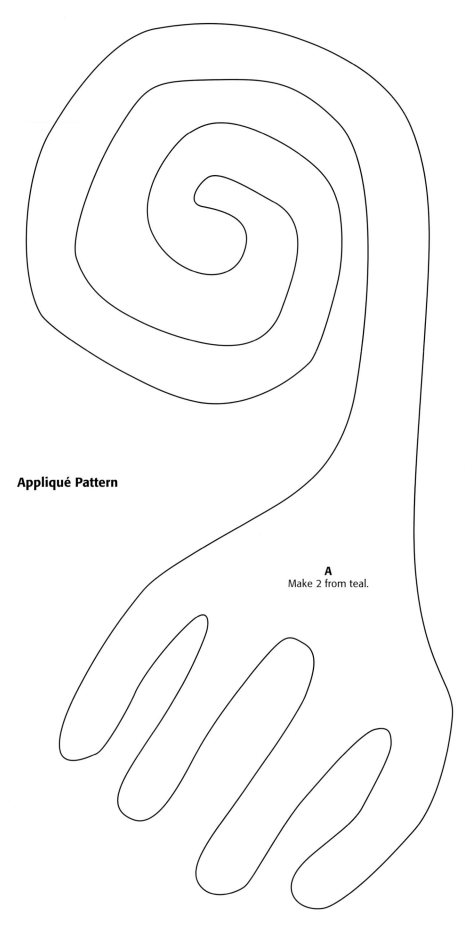

Appliqué Pattern

A
Make 2 from teal.

Appliqué Patterns

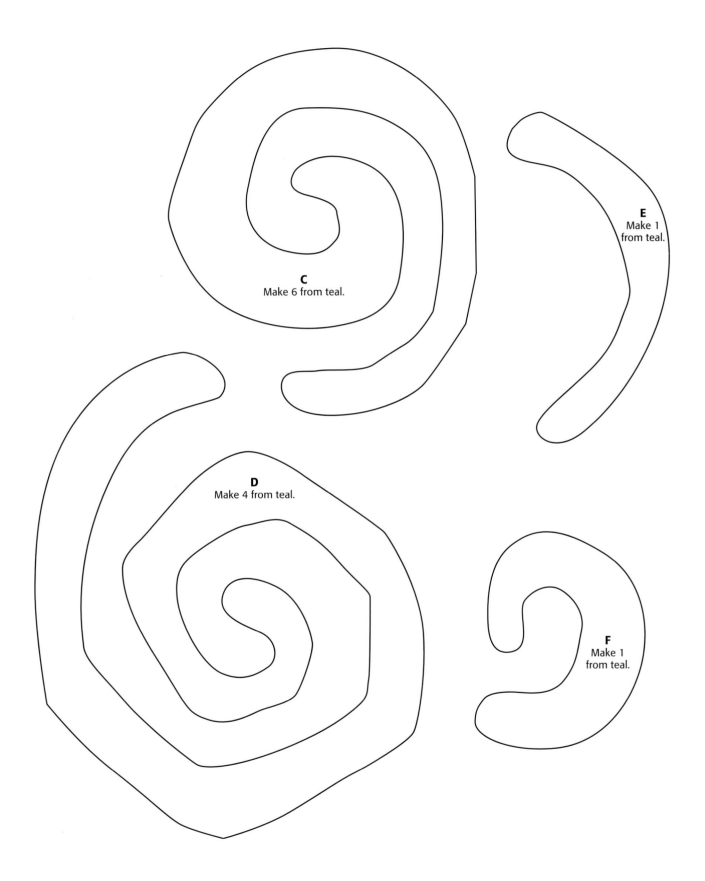

C
Make 6 from teal.

E
Make 1
from teal.

D
Make 4 from teal.

F
Make 1
from teal.

Cascade Cabins

By Mary Hickey. Quilted by Judy Irish.

These simple little blocks take on a whimsical quality with their goofy tilted corners. The quilt is both naive and sophisticated at the same time. The blocks are very easy to construct, the quilt is quick to make, and the end result provides a strong, humorous statement.

Finished quilt size: 52" x 52"
Finished block size: 8" x 8"

Materials

Yardages are based on 42"-wide fabrics.

- 1⅜ yards of beige polka-dot fabric for block backgrounds and middle border
- ⅝ yard of medium green print for Tilting Cabin block corners
- ⅝ yard of dark green solid for Tilting Tree block corners
- ¾ yard of dark green print for outer border
- ½ yard *total* of assorted green fabrics for trees
- ½ yard *total* of assorted brown fabrics for roofs and tree trunks
- ⅜ yard of black solid for inner border
- ¼ yard *each* of 3 assorted rust fabrics for cabins
- ⅛ yard of gold print for cabin doors
- 3⅜ yards of fabric for backing
- ⅞ yard of fabric for binding
- 56" x 56" piece of batting

Cutting

All measurements include ¼"-wide seam allowances.

From *each* of 2 of the 3 assorted rust fabrics, cut:

2 rectangles, 2" x 12"

1 strip, 1½" x 20"; crosscut into 4 rectangles, 1½" x 4½"

From the remaining assorted rust fabric, cut:

2 rectangles, 2" x 15"

1 strip, 1½" x 25"; crosscut into 5 rectangles, 1½" x 4½"

From the gold print, cut:

1 strip, 1½" x 42"; crosscut into:

2 rectangles, 1½" x 12"

1 rectangle, 1½" x 15"

From the beige polka-dot fabric, cut:

4 strips, 3½" x 42"; crosscut into:

26 squares, 3½" x 3½"

26 rectangles, 1½" x 3½"

2 strips, 1½" x 42"; crosscut into 12 rectangles, 1½" x 6½"

2 strips, 6¼" x 42"; crosscut into 12 squares, 6¼" x 6¼"

1 strip, 2½" x 42"; crosscut into 2 strips, 2½" x 21"

5 strips, 2" x 42"

From the assorted brown fabrics, cut a *total* of:

3 strips, 3½" x 42"; crosscut into 13 rectangles, 3½" x 6½"

1 strip, 1½" x 21"

From the medium green print, cut:

6 strips, 3" x 42"; crosscut into 26 rectangles, 3" x 7⅛"

From the assorted green fabrics, cut a *total* of:

12 squares, 5⅞" x 5⅞"

From the dark green solid, cut:
5 strips, 3" x 42"; crosscut into 24 rectangles,
 3" x 7⅛"

From the black solid, cut:
5 strips, 2" x 42"

From the dark green print, cut:
6 strips, 3¼" x 42"

From the binding fabric, cut:
218" of 2¼"-wide bias strips

Assembling the Tilting Cabin Blocks

1. Stitch matching 2" x 12" rust rectangles to both long sides of a 1½" x 12" gold rectangle as shown. Make two strip sets. Crosscut *each* strip set into four segments, 2½" wide. Stitch the 2" x 15" rust rectangles to both long sides of the 1½" x 15" gold rectangle. Crosscut the strip set into five segments, 2½" wide.

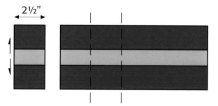

2. Sew a matching 1½" x 4½" rust rectangle to the tops of each segment from step 1 as shown.

3. Stitch a 1½" x 3½" polka-dot rectangle to the sides of the units from step 2 as shown.

4. Using a pencil and your rotary-cutting ruler, draw a diagonal line from corner to corner on the wrong side of each 3½" polka-dot square. Place a marked square on one end of each of the 3½" x 6½" brown rectangles as shown. Stitch on the marked line. Trim ¼" from the stitching line. Flip the polka-dot triangle up and press the seam toward the brown. Repeat on the opposite end of the brown rectangle, positioning the marked square as shown.

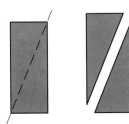

5. Stitch each unit from step 4 to a unit from step 3 as shown to make the cabin units.

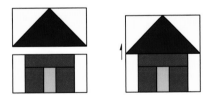

6. Cut each of the 3" x 7⅛" medium green rectangles in half diagonally as shown to make 52 triangles. Be sure to make the cut from the upper-right corner to the lower-left corner.

7. Stitch a triangle from step 6 to the top and bottom of each cabin unit as shown. Press the seams toward the triangles. Stitch a triangle to each side of each cabin unit. Press the seams toward the triangles. Make 13 Tilting Cabin blocks.

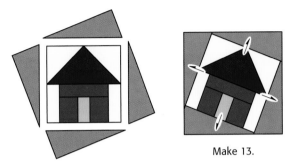

Make 13.

Assembling the Tilting Tree Blocks

1. Fold each of the 5⅞" assorted green squares in half, wrong sides together. Cut each folded square diagonally from fold to corner as shown. Discard the two triangles cut from the right side. Unfold the remaining triangle. This will be the tree.

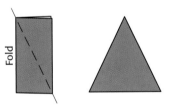

2. Fold each of the 6¼" polka-dot squares in half, wrong sides together. Cut each folded square diagonally from fold to corner as shown. Discard the folded triangle. The two triangles cut from the right side will be the tree background pieces.

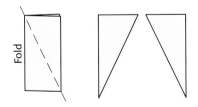

3. Stitch the triangles from step 2 to the sides of the green triangle from step 1 as shown. Press the seams toward the green.

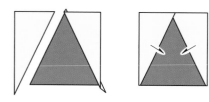

4. Stitch a 2½" x 21" polka-dot strip to both long sides of the 1½" x 21" brown strip. Crosscut the strip set into 12 segments, 1½" wide.

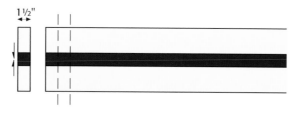

5. Sew a segment from step 4 to each tree unit as shown. Stitch a 1½" x 6½" polka-dot rectangle to the left side of each tree unit.

6. Cut each of the 3" x 7⅛" dark green solid rectangles in half diagonally as shown to make 48 triangles. Be sure to make the cut from the upper-left corner to the lower-right corner.

7. Stitch a triangle from step 6 to the top and bottom of each tree unit as shown. Press the seams toward the triangles. Stitch a triangle to each side of each tree unit. Press the seams toward the triangles. Make 12 Tilting Tree blocks.

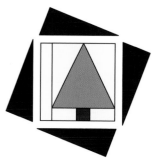
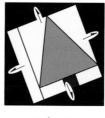

Make 12.

Assembling the Quilt Top

1. Refer to the photograph on page 104 to arrange the blocks in five horizontal rows of five blocks each as shown, alternating the blocks within each row and from row to row.

2. Stitch the blocks in each row together; press the seams toward the Tilting Tree blocks. Stitch the rows together; press the seams in one direction.

3. Refer to "Borders with Straight-Sewn Corners" on page 8 to join and trim the black strips to the correct lengths and stitch them to the quilt top. Press the seams toward the border strips. Repeat with the 2" x 42" polka-dot strips for the middle border and the 3¼" x 42" dark green print strips for the outer border.

Finishing the Quilt

Refer to "Quiltmaking Techniques" on page 5 for details on quilt finishing, if needed.

1. Cut and piece the backing fabric so it is approximately 4" to 6" larger than the quilt top.

2. Layer the backing, batting, and quilt top; baste the layers together.

3. Hand or machine quilt as desired. The quilt shown was machine quilted with pine branches, roof tiles, leaves, outlines, and spirals.

4. Trim the batting and backing even with the quilt top. Make a hanging sleeve and attach it to the quilt back.

5. Bind the quilt edges with the bias strips. Add a label to the quilt back.

Fireside Blanket

By Mary Hickey. Quilted by Dawn Kelly.

This Native American–style quilt is made up of two different blocks, the Longhouse and an alternate block. The center of each Longhouse block is a modified Log Cabin surrounded by half-square triangles. The alternate block is just a simple square with two triangles and a square in the middle. The instructions tell you where to put which color. You can follow the directions, or you could combine colors at random and the quilt might look even better. "Fireside Blanket" is both masculine and cheerful. The solid colors give it a little more dignity than the usual cottage quilt.

Finished quilt size: 44½" x 55¾"
Finished block size: 8" x 8"

Materials

Yardages are based on 42"-wide fabrics.

- 2⅞ yards of navy blue solid for block backgrounds, setting triangles, and outer border
- ¾ yard of bright red solid for blocks and inner border
- ⅝ yard of light blue solid for blocks
- ½ yard of rust solid for blocks
- ½ yard of yellow solid for blocks
- ½ of yard of green solid for blocks
- Scrap of brown solid, no smaller than 10" x 10", for blocks
- Scrap of medium blue solid, no smaller than 5" x 10", for blocks
- Scrap of maroon solid, no smaller than 5" x 10", for blocks
- Scrap of reddish orange solid, no smaller than 4" x 4", for blocks
- 3 yards of fabric for backing
- ⅞ yard of fabric for binding
- 49" x 60" piece of batting

Cutting

All measurements include ¼"-wide seam allowances.

From the navy blue solid, cut:

6 squares, 12" x 12"

2 strips, 1" x 42"; crosscut into 6 rectangles, 1" x 8"

3 strips, 1½" x 42"; crosscut into:

    24 squares, 1½" x 1½"

    24 rectangles, 1½" x 2½"

3 strips, 2½" x 42"; crosscut into:

    24 squares, 2½" x 2½"

    12 rectangles, 2½" x 3½"

3 strips, 3½" x 42"; crosscut into:

    12 squares, 3½" x 3½"

    12 rectangles, 3½" x 5½"

3 squares, 12¾" x 12¾"; cut each square in half twice diagonally to yield 12 side setting triangles. You will use 10 and have 2 left over.

2 squares, 6¾" x 6¾"; cut each square in half once diagonally to yield 4 corner setting triangles

5 strips, 4¼" x 42"

From the light blue solid, cut:

2 squares, 12" x 12"

2 strips, 1½" x 42"; crosscut into:
    8 squares, 1½" x 1½"
    8 rectangles, 1½" x 2½"
    8 rectangles, 1½" x 4½"
    1 rectangle, 1½" x 8"

8 squares, 2" x 2"

From the green solid, cut:

1 square, 12" x 12"

1 rectangle, 1½" x 8"

4 squares, 1½" x 1½"

4 squares, 2" x 2"

4 rectangles, 1½" x 2½"

4 rectangles, 1½" x 4½"

2 squares, 2½" x 2½"

From the yellow solid, cut:

1 square, 12" x 12"

4 squares, 1½" x 1½"

8 squares, 2" x 2"

From the bright red solid, cut:

1 square, 12" x 12"

8 squares, 2" x 2"

4 squares, 1½" x 1½"

5 strips, 1¾" x 42"

From the rust solid, cut:

1 square, 12" x 12"

1 rectangle, 1½" x 8"

8 squares, 2" x 2"

2 squares, 2½" x 2½"

From the brown solid, cut:

2 squares, 2½" x 2½"

4 rectangles, 1½" x 2½"

4 rectangles, 2½" x 4½"

From the maroon solid, cut:

4 rectangles, 1½" x 2½"

4 rectangles, 2½" x 4½"

From the medium blue solid, cut:

4 rectangles, 1½" x 2½"

4 rectangles, 1½" x 4½"

From the reddish orange solid, cut:

4 squares, 1½" x 1½"

From the binding fabric, cut:

213" of 2¼"-wide bias strips

Assembling the Longhouse Blocks

1. Refer to "Half-Square-Triangle Units" on page 5 to make the half-square triangles. Pair a 12" navy blue square with each light blue, green, yellow, red, and rust 12" square. Cut the strips 2½" wide. Cut from each color combination the number of squares indicated.

Make 32.   Make 16.   Make 16.   Make 16.   Make 16.

2. Stitch the half-square triangles into pairs as shown, making half of the pairs in each color combination with the triangles in the opposite direction.

3. Stitch a navy blue 1" x 8" rectangle to both long edges of the light blue, rust, and green 1½" x 8" rectangles. Crosscut *each* strip set into four segments, 1½" wide.

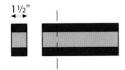

1½"

4. Stitch a 1½" x 2½" navy blue rectangle to the sides of each segment as shown.

5. Stitch a 1½" x 2½" light blue rectangle to the top and bottom of two units from step 4 with a green center square and two units with a rust center square as shown. Stitch a 1½" x 4½" light blue rectangle to the sides of these units. In the same manner, refer to the illustration to make two units *each* of the remaining color combinations, using the brown, green, maroon, and medium blue rectangles.

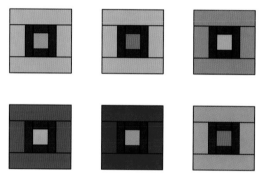

Make 2 of each.

6. Using a pencil and your rotary-cutting ruler, draw a diagonal line from corner to corner on the wrong side of each 2" light blue, rust, green, red, and yellow square. Set aside four yellow, four light blue, and four red squares for use in the alternate blocks. Place each of the remaining marked squares on one corner of each 2½" navy blue square as shown. Stitch on the marked lines. Trim ¼" from the stitching line. Flip open the triangles and press the seams toward the navy blue squares.

Make 24 total.

7. Stitch each 1½" red, yellow, light blue, green, and reddish orange square to a 1½" navy square. Stitch a 1½" x 2½" navy blue rectangle to the sides of the pairs as shown.

Make 24 total.

8. Arrange four matching half-square-triangle units from step 2, one unit from step 5, two units from step 6, and two units from step 7 into three horizontal rows as shown. Stitch the units in each row together and then stitch the rows together to complete the Longhouse blocks.

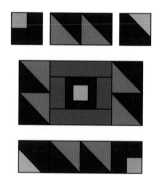

Make 12.

Assembling the Alternate Blocks

1. Place the squares you marked previously in step 6 of "Assembling the Longhouse Blocks" on the corners of the 3½" navy blue squares, right sides together, as shown. Stitch on the marked lines. Trim ¼" from the stitching line. Flip open the triangles and press the seams toward the navy blue squares.

Make 12 total.

2. Arrange two different-colored squares from step 1, two 3½" x 5½" navy blue rectangles, two 2½" x 3½" navy blue rectangles, and one 2½" rust, green, or brown square into three horizontal rows as shown. Stitch the pieces in each row together and then stitch the rows together to complete the alternate blocks.

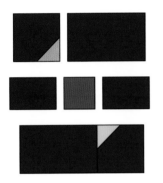

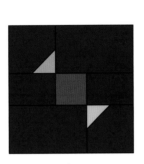

Make 6.

Quilt Assembly

Assembling the Quilt Top

1. Refer to the quilt assembly diagram to arrange the Longhouse blocks, the alternate blocks, and the side setting triangles into diagonal rows as shown.

2. Stitch the pieces in each row together; press the seams toward the setting triangles and alternate blocks. Stitch the rows together; press the seams in one direction. Add the corner setting triangles to each corner.

3. Refer to "Borders with Straight-Sewn Corners" on page 8 to join and trim the 1¾" x 42" red strips to the correct lengths and stitch them to the quilt top. Press the seams toward the setting triangles. Repeat with the 4¼" x 42" navy blue strips for the outer border. Press the seams toward the navy blue strips.

Finishing the Quilt

Refer to "Quiltmaking Techniques" on page 5 for details on quilt finishing, if needed.

1. Cut and piece the backing fabric so it is approximately 4" to 6" larger than the quilt top.

2. Layer the backing, batting, and quilt top; baste the layers together.

3. Hand or machine quilt as desired. The quilt shown was machine quilted with zigzags and spirals.

4. Trim the batting and backing even with the quilt top. Make a hanging sleeve and attach it to the quilt back.

5. Bind the edges with the bias strips. Add a label to the quilt back.

About the Author

Mary Hickey has been a bestselling author, a teacher, and an influential leader in the quilting world for more than twenty-five years. She continually brings new ideas to quiltmaking, focusing her energies on creating fresh-looking designs, clever techniques, and traditional patterns. As a master designer, her primary goal is to create projects and write instructions that enable quiltmakers to create beautiful, traditional quilts that look complex, artistic, and stunning but that are easy to make.

Mary lives in the Northwestern coastal area of Washington State where she thoroughly enjoys her family, especially her first grandchild, Audrey. She loves listening to baseball, opera, and books on tape while stitching on her porch swing and watching the birds, seals, and other wildlife in Liberty Bay.